D1626330

As Time Goes By

About Alice Taylor's other books

And Time Stood Still
'Warmed my heart and reminded me of the value of family,
friendship and community.' *Irish Independent*

Tea and Talk
'A delight.'
The Sean O'Rourke Show, RTÉ Radio 1

Do You Remember?
'Magical … Reading the book, I felt a faint ache in my heart … I find
myself longing for those days … This book is important social history …
remembering our past is important. Alice Taylor has given us a handbook
for survival. In fact, it is essential reading.'
Irish Independent

And Life Lights Up
'Alice's beautiful and captivating writing is an act of mindfulness in itself,
and she shares her favourite moments in life, encouraging us to ponder
our own. Alice also inspires the reader to be attentive to the here and now
and embrace moments as they arise. A beautiful and enchanting book by a
bestselling and celebrated author.'
Mummypages

For more books by Alice Taylor, see www.obrien.ie

Alice Taylor has lived in the village of Innishannon since 1961 and documented village life over the years, especially in her books *The Village* and *The Parish*.

In this book, through the prism of one year, she looks at life in today's Ireland and the efforts of her village to maintain a sense of identity and of a vibrant, caring community as it spreads from a quiet, tranquil oasis out to many new housing estates, and through it a hub of throbbing traffic constantly passes.

RECENT BOOKS BY ALICE TAYLOR

And Time Stood Still

The Gift of a Garden

Do You Remember?

The Women

Tea and Talk

Home for Christmas

And Life Lights Up

As Time Goes By

Alice Taylor

Photographs by Emma Byrne

First published 2019 by Brandon,
an imprint of The O'Brien Press
12 Terenure Road East, Rathgar,
Dublin 6, DO6 HD27, Ireland
Tel: +353 1 4923333; Fax: +353 1 4922777
E-mail: books@obrien.ie
Website: www.obrien.ie
The O'Brien Press is a member of Publishing Ireland.

ISBN 978-1-78849-137-2

Text copyright © Alice Taylor 2019
Photographs © Emma Byrne, except for photographs of St
Mel's Cathedral, which are used by kind permission of Bishop
Colm O'Reilly and Tiernan Dolan, and picture of geese on
page 22, which is used by kind permission of Bex Sheridan.
Typesetting, editing, layout, design © The O'Brien Press Ltd.

10 9 8 7 6 5 4 3 2 1
23 22 21 20 19

Printed and bound in Poland by
Białostockie Zakłady Graficzne S.A.
The paper in this book is produced using pulp from
managed forests.

Published in:

Dedication

In memory of my father,
who planted trees, nurtured his land and the wildlife on
it and advised us not to upset the balance of nature.

Contents

Introduction

The joy of anticipation
Awaiting dreams' realisation
Looking forward is the fun
Of happy things yet to come.

We open the door into a New Year with a certain sense of anticipation. This anticipation is the pearl within the oyster of our lives which lights up the present and gives a beckoning forward finger to the future. It entices us on with a sense of hope in our hearts and brings an added glow to our lives. Maybe it is one of the reasons why we should plant a few uplifting experiences into the year ahead to which we can look forward with a sense of excitement in our hearts.

Children are masters of the art of anticipation as they look forward to Santa, their birthdays and holidays. They pack huge enjoyment into occasions before they ever happen. As we grow older we may lose that sense of anticipation. Perhaps standing on the threshold of a new year is a good time to rekindle the flame. That is why at the beginning of 2018 I put two places to visit on my bucket list.

Then, as the year unfolded it turned up some surprises of its own. It was the year of the Big Snow. The year of the Scorching Heat Wave. The year of the Pope. For me and probably for you 2018 was a mixture of many things.

However, for me 2018 was an extra special year because I had a big birthday on the horizon, though my birthdays have always been occasions to which I have given very little attention. Birthdays in our family were never the cause of any great excitement. They came and went without too much notice being paid to them. This year, however, with a big one on the horizon, everyone felt that we should do something special to mark the occasion. But I was quite prepared to let this birthday like all the others pass me by with the minimum of fuss – and warned all around me that the last thing I wanted was a surprise birthday party or any such thing. How lacking in a sense of occasion and anticipation was that?

Still, maybe it was this big birthday that caused me to decide in January 2018 to write about the happenings of the year as they unfolded. Big things and little things. The book would depend on what the year brought along.

Also, in January the *Captain's Log* kicked me into introducing a sense of a planned voyage into my life, and then a goose that arrived late for Christmas got me sizzling. And so the year rolled out, unfolding the ordinary and the extraordinary. When the Big Snow whirled in during March many people had never before seen the likes of it. But for me it brought back childhood memories of 1947, the year of the last Big Snow.

Back then we had never heard of double glazing and the bitter cold seeped in through rattling windows and under draughty doors, and we gathered around the kitchen fire with our coats on to keep warm. That snow lasted for many, many weeks and blanketed the entire country under huge six-foot-deep drifts. The burning heatwave which followed in July was the same pattern as 2018. But seventy years ago there were no water shortages as back then very few homes had a piped water supply and on the farm the heatwave did not affect the natural water supply of springs and wells from the depths of the land. Last year, however, it was a different story and for the first time many of us had to become water-use conscious. A water-hose ban came into place, a new experience for us Irish.

Then the Pope came to Ireland for the World Meeting

of Families and one wonders how he will remember our 'céad míle fáilte'. Donald Trump strutted his stuff on the world stage while Stormont kept its curtains closed. We in the South prayed that common sense would prevail as we watched with consternation the Brexit debate convulse our nearest neighbours in Westminster into total disarray. If they jumped blindly overboard the backwash could have dire consequences for us.

In the meantime, here in Innishannon life went on and we celebrated many milestones. The Parish Hall was built by voluntary labour in 1968, an inconceivable achievement in today's world, and was now fifty years in action. Our local Tidy Towns group got going that year as well, which was ten years after the establishment of the national Tidy Towns organisation which has contributed in no small way to the development of Irish tourism. Like many other places in rural Ireland, both the Parish Hall and Tidy Towns have enriched parish living over the years. Our annual Christmas magazine, *Candlelight*, was in its 35th edition of recording the observations and remembrances of our parish. Many other parishes have similar publications, and what a valuable historical archive they are for each place.

Also, I got to visit two places that were on my bucket list: St Mel's Cathedral in Longford and

Ballyfin demesne in County Laois, one catering for the divine and the other the human – but both food for the body and soul. And to a place of total self-indulgence, Kelly's of Rosslare! All these places were a joy to visit.

So come back with me to 2018 and enjoy some of the big events and also some of the funny, quirky little things and unexpected surprises that are all part of everyday living as time goes by.

The Captain's Log

Do you believe in New Year resolutions? I am never quite sure how to answer that question. Maybe every New Year I do have vague intentions of getting certain things done, but I never quite follow up on them. But this year fate stepped in and I was hauled on board a very committed direct line.

In the dying days of 2017 I was attending an Anthony De Mello day in the Nano Nagle Centre in Mallow and after lunch, while I was collecting a cup of tea from a self-service table, a pleasant woman standing beside me asked, 'Did you know Dan and Nellie Brown?', referring to a couple from my childhood home town. 'Oh yes,' I told her, 'they had the corner shop in our town.' And that was the sum total of our chat!

However, a few weeks later, a packet wrapped in good-quality cardboard arrived in the post. The wrapping was pretty impressive and gave the sense of something important within. So I cautiously eased a small, pointed knife along the edges, careful not to damage whatever was inside. Then I gently took out the contents. It was a book. But this was no ordinary book. It was a book bound in soft, rich brown leather. Embossed in gold into the cover was the image of a ship's anchor. Holding the book closed was an elegant, elasticated brown ribbon attached to the top and bottom of the back and stretching comfortably around the front cover. Wrapped over the lower half of the book, linking the front to the back cover, was a band of glossy, rich golden paper. On this paper was the emblem of a ship's steerage wheel, and under it was printed 'The Captain's Log'. Beneath that, in smaller print: 'A journal for Life's Journey'. Protruding from the base of the book were three bookmarks, colour-coordinated in a rich brown, gold and cream. The entire production was a tastefully blended, elegant object. I ran my hands gently and slowly over this lovely leather creation. It felt gorgeous! It was an impressive production. But what was it all about?

Before opening the book, I examined it carefully and at the back, on the golden flap, was printed the following: 'A simple structured journal that helps you strike a balance between being productive and just being.' It listed the contents and aims of the journal. The aims were to help you:

Live with purpose
Set meaningful goals

Cultivate gratitude
Build positive habits
Stay motivated and productive.

'Wow!' I gasped. Was all this possible? Sounded great, but how was all this supposed to happen? But I was to learn that 'happen' was the wrong word, 'be accomplished' would have been a better description. Full of curiosity, I opened up this amazing book that promised so much. Inside was a note from the woman I had met in Mallow, telling me that her son had compiled *The Captain's Log*. On the very first page was a space for your name giving you an immediate sense of ownership. Then came an arresting quote from 'Invictus', by William Ernest Henley:

It matters not how strait the gate,
How charged with punishments the scroll,
I am the master of my fate,
I am the captain of my soul.

Then a page that left you under no illusions as to who was responsible for the success of this voyage. It spelt it out:

'The captain's log has been used for centuries on the high seas to help determine the direction a ship has travelled. It was an essential tool for the ship's navigation and was filled in daily. Similarly, this journal can be a useful tool for your journey through life. Here you are the captain and if you want to move forward in life, what could be more valuable than knowing who you are, the path that you're on and your strategy for getting there? This is what the captain's log aims to help you answer.'

'Aye, Aye, Captain!'

Then came some pages of profound wisdom, quoting sages and philosophers from the past and indeed the present. It made for very stimulating reading.

Then came the hard bit, the plan for your own voyage. This basically consisted of a monthly, weekly and daily plan for the next six months. You decided on what it was you desired most to achieve in your life; you set out your plan and then kept a daily, weekly and monthly record. The secret was to plan your priorities each night and to structure your day with your priorities in mind, beginning in the morning: 'Win the morning and you win the day.'

I read it a few times to come to grips with the whole thing. It made for fascinating reading, but it was a daunting undertaking and not for the faint-hearted. It claimed that in order for any undertaking to become a habit, you had to do it between twenty-one and sixty-six times, and then it became

Waiting
for the
snow

Snow
here

Meditation
Walking
~Less Judging and living
Get to bed 9.30
Get up at 8am
Eat more fruit
⓪ Drink more water

REVIEW
(Use the questions on the tip sheet as prompts if needed)

The first day of Spring. A month in
my voyage with the Captain's log. Is it
making a difference? I think so. The medita...
is slowly becoming a habit. and makin...
big effort. With walking. The writing
is flowing. Happy with that

15 FEB Is the Captain's log making a difference?
It is definetly making a difference I...
my writing and I am getting in more
meditation. I think that 91-1 is bringing
more focus

20th FEB. Struggling to keep up with it. but-
making a big effort. Went off the tracks with
...day everything. Amazing day
...impulse birthday party. Covered. Had
...h Annan snow birthday
...t. Birthday 🎂

an established habit which you did almost effortlessly. You followed the book faithfully for six months. At the end of the six months you were on course, and you had established your desired outcomes as a regular habit.

This was not a vague voyage on which you set out with no sense of direction. On this voyage you nailed your colours to the mast, then set sail. And it was not a case of 'all hands on deck'. You were the only hands on deck! You were the captain and the crew, and you planned your voyage with meticulous care. Each night you filled in your log so that the following day you were guaranteed to reach your desired destination. There was nothing left to chance. At the end of each week, and again each month, you did a similar assessment. It all made great sense!

But would it work? There was only one way to find out and that was to get on board. So, with my *Captain's Log*, I planned my voyage for the following six months.

On 1 January 2018 I set sail … see you when I land on 1 July.

Goosey, Goosey, Gander

As I was trying to get my head around saying goodbye to the old year, an abandoned goose found her way to me in a rather unusual fashion. She heralded her arrival in through an upstairs bedroom window. If I was an alert captain I would have thrown her overboard.

It was one of those misty, overcast days between the Christmasses when the world waits for its soul to catch up. I crawled, sleepy-headed, out of bed and on glancing through the window to determine the state of the world outside, noticed that the window box on the sill, where the spring primroses and bulbs were attempting to shoulder their way up through the sodden soil, was in the need of some attention. So I opened the window and as I began my rescue operation, a voice from the street below called up, 'Do you want a goose for the Little Christmas?' My neighbour, John, who has a butcher's shop further down the

street was passing by and decided that this might be an opportune moment to offload a leftover Christmas goose.

'A goose?' I questioned.

'Yes, it honks and flaps its wings,' he said giving an impromptu imitation of a waddling goose.

'John, it's too early in the morning to be funny,' I complained.

'Early, how are you! It's nearly the middle of the day. Now, do you want the goose or not?'

'Not sure,' I said reluctantly. 'I'll have to think about that. Don't know that I'm able to face a goose so soon after the Christmas turkey.'

'No comparison,' he assured me. 'A turkey is food for the masses, but a goose is food for the gods.'

'Why did you not suggest a goose to me for Christmas so?' I demanded.

''Tis only now that I have a goose available,' he told me. 'A fella who rears his own geese brought her in to me for a fella who was looking for a goose, but when the shagger who wanted the goose heard the price on Christmas Eve he wouldn't pay it – and I wouldn't give him the satisfaction of a bargain because he is such a mane bastard.'

'Well, that must have been a very interesting exchange,' I told him.

'He was lucky that it was only words we exchanged,'

he told me. 'He was lucky that I didn't clobber him with his bloody goose.'

'So it's a leftover goose I'm getting?'

'Don't you start now,' he cautioned.

'But she is a leftover.'

'She is! But still a fine bird,' he insisted.

'Are you sure, now, that she is not an old gander, by any chance, is she?' I demanded.

'Oh for God's sake,' he wailed.

'But she could be,' I persisted.

'No way!' he declared emphatically. 'She has a big, soft, white bosom, so she is the real deal. All goosey, goosey …'

'Let it with me and I'll think about it,' I told him, closing the window.

I sat on the bed and thought about roast goose. I was reared with geese. I had watched them grow from fluffy goslings to full-bodied matrons, and every Christmas my mother had stuffed and roasted one for Christmas Day, New Year's Day and Little Christmas. I had golden memories of roast goose and the luscious potato stuffing that oozed out her back and front apertures, floating in a waterfall of gorgeous goose grease. A dietician's nightmare, but a divine delicacy for us children who were reared on bacon and cabbage and had no cholesterol complex. That precious memory of roast goose still hung like a golden holly wreath on a back page of my mind. But I had never actually cooked a goose. And maybe sometimes such memories are best left undisturbed to glow in the shrine of childhood! Goldsmith may well have been right:

> Remembrance wakes with all her busy train,
> Swells at my breast, and turns the past to pain.

Could awakening my sleeping golden memory of roast goose turn it into a present-day pain and kill my nostalgic remembrance?

But there is no fool like a nostalgic fool, so before I totally lost myself in the misleading mists of memory I decided to do a reality check – to ring my 'Johnny Sound All'. In life, we all need a Johnny Sound All – this is a person off whom you can bounce your ideas. Other times we need a good listener and sometimes a rage buddy. But there are times when you just need someone to sound a cautionary note when you are in danger of getting carried away on a misleading flood of enthusiasm that could swirl you on to sharp rocks. To avoid such catastrophies it is good to have someone with clear vision, not blinded as you may be by a rush of excitement to the head. My Johnny Sound All is a sister who is sharp of intellect and brutally honest. She is an expert in all things culinary and, if the truth be told, considers herself an expert on almost everything else in life as well. She has often parachuted me out of crash-landings. I ran my goose idea across her.

'When did you last eat roast goose?' she demanded.

'When our mother cooked it many centuries ago,' I told her.

'And now you are suffering from rose-coloured-glasses recall,' she said skeptically, diagnosing my condition in one clear-sighted analysis.

'Could be,' I admitted.

'Well, the only cure for that, I suppose, is to cook your own goose, though in the process you may well kill that goose who laid that golden egg of wonderful memories.'

'I think I might chance it,' I told her doubtfully.

So later that day I went down the street to inspect the goose. A live goose proudly parading around a farmyard is an impressive lady, but strip her of her plumage and a demeaning transformation is effected. The ladies of historic royal courts must have faced the same dilemma nightly when bared of all their finery. On the removal of their elaborately coiffed head-dresses and magnificently layered gowns, they were stripped down to their simple, unadorned bodies. So it was with this goose. There she lay before me, a shadow of her former self, plucked of her glistening white feathers, long neck and flailing wings.

Then, on closer inspection, I decided that she was extremely long of body for a goose and bore a distinct resemblance to the larger frame of a gander.

'I think your goose could be a gander,' I informed John.

'How did you come to that smart conclusion?' he demanded acidly.

'She has the body build of a gander.'

'She has not; she is just a fine, big-bodied goose,' he asserted.

'Well, if she is a goose, she is an old one who has been around for a long time to develop a body like that. With muscles like that she covered a lot of ground in her day. She could be as tough as old shoe leather.'

'Do you want her or don't you?' he demanded impatiently.

'Will I have to pay full whack for her?' I demanded.

'You will. She cost me sixty-five euro so I'm making nothing on her. I was charging the old bollocks who ordered her seventy-five euro and he told me that he had sold geese when he was young for 17 shillings and 6 pence and here was I now trying to charge him seventy-five pounds for one. Can you imagine, he is still stuck in pounds?'

'I can understand that,' I told him.

'Well, I can't. But the question now is, what am I going to do with you?'

'No! The question is what are you going to do with your goose that could be a gander,' I told him.

'It's not a gander,' he persisted and seizing the opportunity to get rid of her, continued, 'if she turns out to be a gander I will give her to you for half price. A deal!'

'But will you take my word for it should I decide that she is a gander?'

'I will,' he agreed, 'because whatever else you might be, you're honest.'

'Well, that's good to know,' I told him.

While this exchange of pleasantries was taking place, a local farmer, whom we both knew, had slipped quietly into the shop and stood silently behind us listening to the exchange.

'What do you think, Tim, is that a goose or a gander?' I asked, seeking a second opinion, although judging by Tim's expression he wished to remain an impartial observer and was in no hurry to get embroiled in controversy.

'Hard to tell. Could be either,' he ventured cautiously, and then, gathering momentum, continued, 'though I do think that she is a bit long-bodied for a young goose. Might have reared a few families. But once she is out of the oven and you stick a fork into her you will know for sure. A young goose is gorgeous, an old goose less so, and a gander – God between us and all harm – would crack your jawbone.'

'When she comes out of the oven is a bit late in the day to be finding all that out,' I told him.

'Well, for God's sake,' John intervened, 'will you take the bloody thing out of my sight whatever she is.'

So I put the goose – who might be a gander – into my basket and bore her – or maybe him – home. Later that night I did a survey on my potential diners. None of them had ever tasted goose and there was unanimous desire to extend their dining palate. So I rang my Johnny Sound All again.

'I have never made potato stuffing, would bread stuffing do?'

'No way! Your mother would turn in her grave.'

'So, how do I make potato stuffing?'

'I sometimes wonder were we reared in the same house, you learnt so little,' she told me.

'Aren't I lucky that you have such great recall,' I told her.

'Listen carefully now! You boil the spuds and peel while still hot and mash with a good dollop of butter and add the breadcrumbs.'

'How much breadcrumbs?' I interrupted.

'Use your head,' I was told.

'Then add onion, apple, thyme, herbs and all the other spices.'

'And that's it?'

'That's it.'

'Same as the other stuffing so, but for the potatoes.'

'Exactly,' she continued, 'but don't put much of the stuffing into the goose because it will be drowned in fat, so put in just a small bit to give flavour, and put an onion and apple into her as well. Put a rack under her in the roasting tin so that she will not be swimming in her own goose grease.'

'Will there be a lot of it?' I asked.

'Just wait and see and listen,' I was told.

Boys oh boys, was she right! As it turned out, my Johnny Sound All was spot-on.

I got my deepest roasting tin and into it put a high rack and laid the goose on top of it, where she sat like a prone monarch lying in state. She was well clear of any waterfall of fat that might begin to flow. Then, very slowly and carefully, I slid the entire menagerie into the Aga oven.

Usually when you thrust anything into the bosom of the Aga she does her work in silence. Not a sound emerges from her deep recesses. She carries out all her activities within her own copious body. A bit like MI5, she works undercover, normally emitting very little evidence of her inner actions. But not on this occasion. Not so! Within minutes of her disappearance into the hot oven the goose began to protest. A ferocious crackling, growling and sizzling began to

explode in the depths of the Aga, so much so that I
was afraid to open the door in case the goose would
shoot out and explode on top of me. An overpowering smell of raging roast began to come forth and the
kitchen filled with a strong aroma. I turned on the
Xpelair at full volume and closed all the kitchen doors
to contain the overpowering smell and prevent the
rest of the house from smelling like a goose cremato-
rium. The Xpelair, however, which is on the window
into the street, broadcast the story of strange happenings within, and shortly afterwards a surprised neighbour opened the kitchen door, sniffing the pungent
air in amazement.

'What the hell are you doing?' she asked. 'I could
get the smell out in the street.'

Then she stood listening to the sounds erupting
from the Aga. 'What have you in there?' she asked.

'A goose,' I told her.

'Sounds like a full-scale raging war is in progress,'
she said. 'It will be interesting to see what will emerge
when that battle is over.'

It would indeed! Eventually I plucked up courage
and gingerly eased open the door of the Aga ever so
slightly. A haze of sizzling fumes engulfed me. There
was fat cascading out through the goose like a glistening waterfall and into the roasting tin already half
full of bubbling fat. The oven was a sizzling inferno. I

slapped the door shut and proceeded to prepare the rest of the dinner, which was scheduled for 4pm – though I am not quite sure that you can call a meal at 4pm 'dinner', but then neither could you call it 'lunch'. The meal which is neither breakfast nor lunch is called 'brunch' so maybe a marriage of lunch and dinner could be a 'lunner'. So let's say we were having lunner at 4pm.

When all the accompaniments were in readiness, the time had come to retrieve the goose. A tricky operation! Moving a crackling goose lying in state on top of a rack standing in a roasting pan of sizzling fat is an exercise requiring precision, balance and extreme caution. A tilt in the wrong direction could have dire consequences. There could be two scorched bodies in the kitchen. But years of experience in removing all kinds of dishes and pans from that Aga oven paid off and the entire concoction landed on the granite worktop by the sink safe from any kind of mishap.

I stood back to survey the body. She was definitely well done. At the time I happened to be reading a historical novel called *A Column of Fire* by Ken Follett, which had been a Christmas gift. Based on the religious struggles between the royal houses of Britain and Europe, it carried graphic descriptions of burning at the stake, which caused me to cringe with horror. My goose bore an uncanny resemblance to those victims.

I took a deep breath and touched her gingerly with a carving knife. Her outer layer cracked open like a suit of armour, revealing a mutilated body within.

When my diners arrived they surveyed the goose with mystified looks on their faces.

Five-year-old Ellie was the first to recover. 'Nana, what is that?' she queried.

'A goose,' I told her.

'Is that what roast goose looks like?' my daughter asked in awe.

'I doubt it,' I told her.

'Is a goose fowl or game?' my son-in-law asked diplomatically.

'This one could be anything,' I told him.

We all sampled her gingerly, but Ellie was the only one to be enthusiastic. 'I love goose,' she proclaimed.

That night my sister rang to inquire about our dining experience. 'Well, was it a goose or a gander?' she asked.

'The answer to that question,' I told her, 'was eroded in the oven.'

'Well, how did it taste?' she wanted to know.

'An experience best forgotten,' I informed her.

Post-Christmas
Low Time

Helen's letter said it all. She was going through a bad patch. It was the beginning of another year and she viewed it as simply 'more of the same'. Her husband was not in the best of health and she had other problems as well, and she was trying, but failing, to stay enthusiastic about living. Because feeling low was not her usual experience of life, this bothered her. She had adult children who were very supportive, and she felt guilty about feeling bad. An old neighbour, excited about his spring bulbs, had called and she envied him his enthusiasm. She wanted to get some enthusiasm back into her own life. She needed a cure for eradicating her winter blues. Life was getting her down. She wanted me to include a chapter in my next book on how to survive a black patch. She suggested that I call it 'Post-Christmas Low Time'. I reread her letter a few times, wondering what to do. Then decided to write back to her as

comfortingly as possible and leave it at that.

But that was easier said than done as her letter stayed rattling around in my head. Her request refused to be forgotten, so I decided to try and do as she asked. I knew exactly what she was talking about and it seemed a bit miserly not to at least try to help. I had no magic recipe, but I could make some effort. As I decided on this course of action, the voice of the late Steve McDonagh, my friend and publisher, echoed back to me: 'Alice, there is a lot of harm done by well-meaning people trying to be helpful.' He was probably right, but on this occasion I was prepared to take a chance.

So what could I do? The only way was to share my own cure for my blue patches. We all have them. Winston Churchill called them the 'black dog on his shoulder'. I call them my 'poor me' days. And sometimes 'poor me' days can hang around longer than they should. But they do pass. When under a black cloud, the belief that it will pass is vital. Easier said than done, I know.

My letter writer was exhausted by life. She was not in a deep depression but felt that things were not as good as they should be. Life was simply getting her down. We have all been there. I was there when I wrote the following:

Defeated

I am weary
And a cold apathy
Oozing through my bones
Makes movement meaningless;
A dead weight
Crushing my mind
Blocks my forward path
And fills my mind with grey.
I could stay here
Motionless forever
In a nook of forgetfulness,
Letting the mainstream course on;
And when the final flood
Would swirl the river down
I would be carried on its crest
Into the final waters beyond.

When I wrote this I was probably exhausted from work and bogged down with small children and a screaming bank manager. And now I cannot even remember what it was that caused me to feel so defeated. Because that cloud lifted and passed on, and life got good again.

When the pace of life was less frantic we had friends who would listen. Now we have counsellors. And both fill a need. I had a friend who lived down the street, and some days as she came in the door I knew by her face that it was a bad day. If I needlessly asked, 'How are you?' I was simply told, 'Shitty.' She said it as it was. That, I think, was a good idea. No pretending that things were other than the way they were.

Then we would sit down and talk. Or rather she talked and I listened, and kept my mouth shut. The choice of subject was hers and it might have nothing to do with what was bothering her. I simply listened. It is vital when you are in a bad place to have a listener, someone non-judgemental who will just sit and listen and keep silent while you are talking – and afterwards not repeat what you said to anybody. That is hugely important. We all need someone safe to listen to us. Someone to whom we can unburden ourselves. Not a 'Johnny Fix It' – they have a different role. In a sad situation Johnny Fix Its can be irritating because some problems can't be fixed, but just talking about them eases the pressure and might help us to see things differently.

But, if at all possible, I think it is better to try to keep that black cloud at bay by taking preventive measures. One friend said to me, 'I have to keep out of that black hole because once I fall in it's brutal hard to get back out.' So, what works for me when the black cloud is threatening? Little things. No big, magic, instant cure, just little things.

Let's begin with the morning. I find a bright, cheery bedroom uplifting. What does your eye fall on first thing in the morning? If you are lucky enough to have a window looking out over a panoramic view at the bottom of your bed, you are blessed. At the bottom of my bed I have a picture of an autumnal woodland scene, with a horse and some pheasants. I love it. If you have an empty wall at the end of your bed, you might hang a picture there. A picture that you like, that brings a smile to your face. And change it occasionally. Because sometimes when things remain the same for too long, we no longer see them. And beneath it on a table, you might put a jug of flowers or a plant. You may think: What the hell difference does that make? But it does. We are all affected by our surroundings. You may not always have fresh flowers, but a pot plant is great too. Or if neither is available, maybe some favourite object that you love and enjoy looking at. I find it really does make a difference.

In the morning as we gradually surface out of sleep, we slowly become aware of our state of mind. If you feel like putting your head under the pillow and negative thoughts filter into your brain, erect a stop sign. Don't go down that road! Don't get on that bus! I find it can help to have a few special books to hand that I can pick up and dip into. It may not be for everybody, but it works for me, and is worth trying. It could be a book of favourite poems or a collection of inspiring quotations. Something positive to start the day. I have one little book that is worn from use. And recently, *Gratias* by John Quinn has joined my bedside collection. It is a dip-into little book, full of comfort and wisdom. I buy these books when out shopping and in good form. That's investing in yourself, a bit like a squirrel putting nuts away for the time when things might not be as good as they are now. If you have them on your bedside table it is surprising what they can do for your morning frame of mind.

At this time of the morning I need to be very careful about turning on the radio. You could have the problems of the world, about which you can do absolutely nothing, flood your mind in a waterfall of negativity. I can't cope with that. I need to be nurtured into wakefulness and gently primed for the day ahead. But if you do feel the need for an outside voice, why not have a favourite CD?

Or how would you feel about keeping a journal? Not a diary, as that is too restricting, but a journal into which you can let your mind meander. Don't plan what you are going to write, just let it happen. It's surprising what will come out and afterwards you will feel much better. Try it! I have kept a journal for years and enjoy it.

Now you are ready to get out of bed. If at all possible, try not to rush – but don't linger too long either unless you are thinking beautiful thoughts. Otherwise you may get bogged down in negativity. Be kind to yourself. If you are having a shower, enjoy it, with wonderful soaps and sponges on hand. Then turn it slowly to cold before you emerge. I'm serious! I do it all the time. It's tough love and not always welcome, but is so stimulating for the mind and body as it gets the circulation going. Afterwards I have wonderful creams to hand for body and foot care. We only get the one body so why not take care of it as there is no replacement, just repairs and maintenance. And maintenance is the first and better option!

If you have a window with a pleasant view in or near your bedroom, have a look out at the world outside. Just outside my bedroom is a door looking out over the garden and some mornings I open it and enjoy gazing out at the trees and inhaling the fresh air. This can be invigorating, especially if you are not feeling up to scratch. We are hugely affected by light, and looking out into a bright day will immediately lift the spirits. If it's a grey, dismal day, forget this.

Once downstairs, have a good breakfast on a well-laid table. This is simply treating yourself with the respect you deserve. If you had a guest, you would treat them well. You deserve no less. For some reason, not known even to myself, I use good china for my weekend breakfasts. It makes me feel that the weekend has more leisure attached to it and gives me a good feeling. Life is all about feeling good within yourself. Now that I am retired I can indulge in all these little comforts, but even when I was on the fast track I would sometimes make the effort to get up early before the racket of the day started and go out into the garden, which was then a bit of a wilderness, and sit and absorb the stillness.

Let me steal five minutes
To welcome in the dawn,
To touch its dewy fingers
As they creep across the lawn.
To watch beneath a misty tree
The sun roll back the night,
Its beams transfusing darkness
With soft translucent light,
To hear the birds awaken
With delight to meet the day
Let their happiness infuse me
To meet my day their way;
Let this tranquil scene give balance
To the busy day ahead,
To create a tranquil pool
For withdrawal inside my head.

I found that once I had that bit of time to myself in the early morning I was then better able to cope with the demands of the day ahead.

I find it wonderful – and necessary – to have at least one very comfortable armchair in which I can relax with ease. A comfort chair. Sounds simple? Amazing how many uncomfortable chairs you sit into in other people's houses. My father, who was not into designer furniture, always advised that an armchair should have an upright, firm back to support your head and shoulders. It would be an extra plus to have one with those shoot-out foot rests to encourage relaxation. Have a few nice, fluffy cushions in your favourite colours. We are very influenced by colour and should surround ourselves with splashes of the colours we like best.

On the wall opposite where you normally sit have a picture that delights you. It does not have to be a masterpiece. I have one of geese on the bank of a river, and I love it. Pleasant pictures around your house are conducive to uplifting, happy thoughts.

I also have a lavender candle that I light on a gloomy day. Lavender is calming to the senses and a lighting candle is comforting. Occasionally I immerse a cut lemon, cloves and a stick of cinnamon in a saucepan of water and bring it to the boil. It cleans the air and fills the house with a pleasant smell. You can re-boil it daily for the same effect. Smells can be very powerful, peaceful and evocative.

It is good to have a lavender eye-cushion, and occasionally take a little time out to lie down on a couch with your eyes covered and listen to your favourite music. For me, instrumental music is less intrusive and more calming than vocal, but this, of course, is purely a matter of choice. We are all different and need to figure out what suits us best. It is so important to have a bit of 'me' time. This is not selfish. It is helping you to help yourself, and then be able to help others if the need arises. There is a wise Chinese proverb that states: 'Stretching herself too far for others she loses herself; the wise woman waters her own garden first.'

If you have a garden or even a tub by the door, go out often and cut flowers, no matter how few there are, and arrange them on the kitchen table. It is amazing how few it takes to make an attractive arrangement. Even the very act of collecting fresh flowers makes you feel good. The touch, the smell and colour all affect our senses. You may not feel like doing it, but kick yourself out the door, and once you get going, the spirits lift. The very sight of the flowers on the table will brighten up your surroundings and make you feel better.

To 'practise what I preach', just after writing this I got up and went out into the garden and collected hellebores, daffodils and some bright yellowish green-ery. There is snow on the ground and the temperature is freezing, but the flowers glow on the table. They make me feel good. If you do not have a garden, why not occasionally spoil yourself by buying a bunch of fresh flowers that you can arrange yourself.

Everybody's day runs differently, but I find it is worthwhile to go for a walk at some stage. Walking releases the happy hormones. While walking, you may also meet people and see things that do you good. If the opportunity arises, take time to stop and have a chat. As Barbra Streisand sang in *Funny Girl*: 'People who need people, are the luckiest people in the world.' Sometime during the day, enjoy a little silence. Our senses are continually battered by sound and we need to give our heads a rest. Too much noise is vexatious to our spirit.

Nighttime! Some people like a warm bedroom, but I am not one of them. I like the bedroom cool, but the bed warm. But it's really all about what suits each of us. I love my electric blanket. We spend a lot of our lives in our beds so we need to make them as welcoming as possible. A well-rested body can cope with life better and also heals itself. Recently I got a gift of a duck down duvet and, oh boy, what a joy! It is like sleeping in a warm bubble. It's made of cotton and filled with duck down from ducks reared on the

JOHN MORIARTY
JANE AUSTEN
DAVID NOKES
REBECCA FRASER
CHARLOTTE BRONTË
ROSAMUNDE
PILCHER
SEPTEMBER
ANOTHER VIEW
THE EMPTY HOUSE
THE PENGUIN BOOK OF IRISH POETRY
DEEPAK CHOPRA
THE SEVEN SPIRITUAL LAWS OF SUCCESS
Moments
Early Poems by Robert Frost
Early Poems by Robert Frost

Silver Hill Duck farm in Monaghan; the duvets are actually made on the farm too. I love it. Now I have invested in two pillows from the same place. Divine! Soft, warm and comforting.

I find that all these little things help to prevent grey days coming my way and if they get in despite all my strategies, a 'listening buddy' is a great help. Not a Johnny Fix It, just somebody who will listen silently and who will bury what they hear in a deep hole of oblivion. They are gold dust in any life. But in order to have good friends you must be a good friend. It works both ways, and friendship, like a garden, has to be cared for and cultivated. How true is this quote from Ralph Waldo Emerson: 'Go oft to the house of thy friend, for weeds choke the unused path.' And don't you love people in life who are prepared to go the extra mile? They enrich all our days.

We all need special tools in life to handle a day when the sun refuses to shine. And each of us has to go through the process of working out what works best for us. Sometimes it's all about the little things – and little things can help a lot.

Marmalade
Making

As the days of January lengthen, marmalade oranges begin to roll around in my head. They are shouting: We've arrived, we're here, come and get us. It is that time of year again. I have a love/hate relationship with marmalade oranges, but the love of homemade marmalade always wins out.

Recently I learned that marmalade making has an old history, with its origins stretching back to the sixteenth century when it was created by Mary Queen of Scots' physician as he mixed oranges and sugar to help ease her sea sickness. Then later, when it became known that vitamin C prevented scurvy, it became a staple diet on seafaring ships. Fresh fruit would not last on long sea voyages but when preserved with sugar it provided a more varied diet for sailors. The threat of scurvy has long gone, but the art of marmalade making, which evolved from its eradication, has lived on. Many centuries later, a nun in Drishane convent,

who had the impressive title of Madame St Benignus, which we pupils abbreviated to Benny, introduced me to the mastery of properly made marmalade. In retrospect, I realise that Benny definitely had a *Captain's Log* mentality! She left nothing to chance and ran a tight ship. Her marmalade making was planned with rigorous precision. She had a *Captain's Log* printed into her brain!

I was dispatched back to Drishane for a year at the age of 17, where my mother felt I would be furnished with skills to enrich my life. I'm not sure that she really had it all thought out in precise detail, but that was probably more or less what she had in mind. In any case, that is exactly what happened.

Amongst the many things they taught us was the art of practical home-making and what my Johnny Sound All ironically terms 'good Protestant housekeeping'! At the time I thought: Who needs to know all this? But life teaches you many things, and probably one of the most important is the art of appreciation. One of the culinary arts instilled in us was the ability to make marmalade, which I then considered a pure waste of time. After all, you could buy a pot of marmalade in any shop. It took me years to appreciate what those dedicated nuns drummed into my uninterested head. I had a lot to learn!

But back to the marmalade making. Like so many

things in life, the thought of doing it is worse than the reality, and once you get going it can, like any creative experience, be deeply satisfying. But it is by far the most complicated and long-drawn-out of all jam-making processes because it has to be done in slow stages. Like all seasonal fruit, you have to do it within a certain timescale and the time for marmalade oranges is January. All other jam making is usually confined to the summer and autumn months, so marmalade is a bit of a maverick. Most fruit used for jam is home grown, but the marmalade oranges come from Seville and the picking of them in sunny Spain must happen around Christmas. So, just when we in Ireland are bracing ourselves to face the harsh weather of the New Year, the golden Spanish oranges sail into our shops. Very different to ordinary oranges, they are smaller and a bit wizened-looking, extremely bitter and packed with pips, which are the setting agent. Unlike other oranges, they are not at this stage very appetising.

Until recent years many people made their own marmalade, so you could buy your required amount of oranges. But not anymore. When I inquired about them this year I was told that I would have to take a full box because if I just took a small amount the shop could not sell the remainder. It was a case of all or nothing. When I told one of my sons this, he informed that this proved that the only ones now making marmalade were geriatrics – people off Noah's Ark. I qualify on that front! And Protestants, he added. I did not qualify there, but the nuns had instilled the Protestant work ethic in me, hadn't they?

So, home came a full box of oranges – too much for me, but there is a solution to most problems. The solution here was a niece who is also a marmalade maker. We split the box of thirty-two pounds of oranges between us, which left me with sixteen pounds. Still a little too much for me, but there is never a shortage of candidates for the surplus marmalade. People love homemade marmalade, but they think it is too much trouble to make. I went through that phase a few years back and then had occasion to go into the Bon Secours hospital in Cork where the nuns were still in action, and still making homemade marmalade. I came home wondering why I had ever given up on it. So I began again.

Sixteen pounds of oranges need to be divided into two jam-making sessions of eight pounds per session. Or four sessions of four pounds per session. The four pounds per session is probably the best option, as the faster you make marmalade the better the flavour, colour and quantity. After years of practice I have worked out a simple system that makes things as easy as possible. The first step is to lay out your requirements with a bit of law and order. An extremely large stainless steel saucepan is a great asset – something I did not have until my wise sister Ellen gave one to me one Christmas. It is a real blessing. Beside this goes the liquidiser, the arrival of which has taken a great deal of the hardship out of marmalade making. Before it came on the scene there was a lot of hand-slicing or using a mincer. Next requirement is a deep bowl or jug lined with a muslin cloth, and the cloth needs to be big enough to drape well over the edge of the container.

As you can see, I still think in the old measure-ments, but all the new utensils have the new, metric measurements and in the old containers the guide-lines have been worn away by time. No problem in today's world. Google has the answer to everything. Recently, when I asked my daughter how many litres there were in six pints of water, she simply picked up her mobile phone and asked it: 'Google, how many litres in six pints of water?' and back came an instant answer. I was impressed! Pity that Google cannot make marmalade ...

The first step is to remove the pips from each orange, which entails cutting each one open right across the middle for easy access to the pips, and then extracting them with a kitchen devil knife – or your fingers, which actually do a better job. You perform this operation over a deep plate or a bowl to catch the resulting flow of juice. Then put the pips and juice into the muslin-lined bowl. Then the gutless oranges go into the liquidiser and when they are shredded to your satisfaction you pour the liquidised contents into the saucepan. You can fit about two gutted oranges into an ordinary liquidiser, so you gradually work your way down through the pile.

Then it is the turn of the lemons. You will need four lemons with four pounds of oranges and eight lemons with eight pounds of oranges. The lemons have far less pips, but their rinds are much tougher than the oranges, so the liquidiser jumps around in protest at their resistance to submission – because of this it is a good idea to mix the lemons and oranges going into the liquidiser. With all the oranges and lemons in the saucepan you then gather up the ends of the overlapping muslin from the bowl, forming a little sack of pips, which you tie firmly with a strong cord. This has to be very secure because were it to break in the cooking the loose pips would ruin your marmalade. You then put this sack of pips into the saucepan and also pour in the juice that has collected beneath it in the bowl. Then, if you are doing four pounds of oranges you pour six pints of water into the saucepan, and double it for eight pounds. Stir well with a wooden spoon. Now, in order to have it properly mixed, you need to get your hand in there to do a right good job! Stage one is now complete.

You leave this to soak overnight, or longer if you wish. One year, due to some distraction, I let it soak for a few days, which gave the oranges a longer period to soften, so they needed less boiling and resulted in better marmalade. A happy accident. But it is a case of whatever works for you!

Now for stage two of the marmalade making. It is probably best to begin this early in the morning as it takes time and if you have an Aga, or any solid-fuel cooker, it needs to be at full heat from the beginning to see you quickly through to the end. Onto the cooker goes the now very heavy saucepan and gradually it comes to the boil. Allow it to simmer until the pectin is extracted from the pips. While this is in progress you need to stir it pretty regularly to avoid the contents sticking to the base as the water content evaporates during the process. To determine when it is ready for the sugar to be added there is a simple test: you warm a little glass and into it put a spoon of the marmalade juice, and when it has cooled you add three teaspoons of methylated spirits. If the juice clots firmly, it is ready for the sugar. This is a crucial point to get right because if you add the sugar too early you will have to over-boil to get the marmalade to set – this darkens the marmalade and reduces the flavour. So you need to make sure that it clots firmly at this point. When it does, you are ready for the sugar. For four pounds of oranges you will need about eight pounds of sugar. Sounds like a lot. It is! And it makes you realise the amount of sugar that goes into all jam.

While the simmering is taking place it is a good idea to line the sugar up along the back of the cooker as warmed sugar dissolves more quickly. Once the sugar is added and dissolved, the secret then is fast boiling. The faster you can get it to reach setting point the nicer your marmalade will taste and look. It will retain its colour and flavour. To test setting point, you put some of the marmalade into a saucer and put it into the fridge to cool. When it forms a firm wrinkle along the top, you are readying for potting.

By now, your saucepan is pretty heavy and you may require extra muscle to shift it from cooker to work-top. You remove the bag of pips, have a pyrex jug on hand for ladling out the jam and line up your jars – the easiest way to prepare your jars is to arrange to have them coming out of the dishwasher at exactly this time, sparkling clean and warm. A few years ago in Ballymaloe shop I picked up a little gadget that is an invaluable asset when filling the jars. It is a little stainless steel, round funnel that sits comfortably on top of all jars, and you simply pour the jam into it and it disappears into the jar without a drip or a smear.

When I saw this I asked myself did I really need such a gadget, which was not exactly cheap, but then I gave myself I good kick in the 'you know where' and brought it home with me. I am so glad that I did! It was worth every penny in the long run and every year as I effortlessly fill my marmalade pots I say: Thank you, Ballymaloe. Once the pots are filled, you can leave the jam to cool and cover later, or you may cover it immediately. Like most things in life there are different schools of thought.

After many years of marmalade making, I have now reached the conclusion that it is best for me to do four pounds of oranges per session, because then the cooking time is much reduced, resulting in a better flavour and nicer colour. With this method, I will have four marmalade sessions, but it's well worth the effort. And while the work is in progress, my kitchen is a haven of tranquility filled with the flow of creativity.

When all is complete and you view the rows of richly glowing pots of marmalade, you get a wonderful sense of satisfaction because there is something deeply calming to the soul in a job well done. The entire marmalade making takes a few hours' work during a few days of January, but for all the other days of the year you have the blessing of beautiful home-made marmalade every morning for your breakfast. Well worth the effort!

Posher than Posh

His father was the master in the local school and when further education was required he was sent away to boarding school instead of going to the small secondary school in the nearby town like the rest of us. When he came home on holidays he regaled us with stories of hunger, hardship and cold. But despite his disparaging accounts about his school, Ballyfin, I sensed that hidden beneath these harrowing details was a certain awe and deep admiration for this isolated, enormous, rambling old mansion that was sited in rolling acres of scenic countryside. His description of this old building that had once seen better days, and was now home to many young students being moulded into future Einsteins, was laced with details of high-ceilinged, draughty rooms and endless, meandering corridors. To me, it sounded like a fascinating place, and into the fertile soil of my teenage imagination went a picture of this decaying mansion and a huge desire to see it.

Time passed by and Ballyfin got buried in the back

pages of my memory. But then one night a few years ago, while I was channel-hopping on the TV, it sprang to life. On rare occasions when you channel-hop late at night you can fall upon a wonderful experience. Not often, but an odd time it can happen. And when it does, you will forever recall the experience with a sense of delight. It is as if you had found the gold nugget in a sieve full of sand.

This happened to me that night when I was putting off climbing the stairs to bed. An old Anglo Irish friend once told me condescendingly, 'The Irish are too lazy to go to bed.' Her comment annoyed the hell out of me at the time, but she could be right! I am a night owl who will sit down at midnight to read a book, the newspaper or turn on the TV to see what the rest of the world is up to. Usually not much, I discover, but on that particular night my channel-hopping paid off. I came on something that I absolutely loved: the restoration of a grand old house. The programme had already begun when I tuned into it so it took me a while to figure out which house was being discussed. To me, the restoration of any old building is a miracle in the making. But this one was a major miracle! And then I realised that it was the restoration of Ballyfin. I was reunited with part of my past and with this place, which I long wondered about but had never seen. I watched and listened in awe.

I learned that this huge old house in the Slieve Bloom Mountains, surrounded by a 600-acre estate, had been designed for the Coote family by architects Richard and William Morrison in 1820. Other great houses had previously stood on the site, including the castle of the O'Mores. In 1820 the great new Ballyfin was regarded as a masterpiece and a wonderful example of the neo-classical style. Here, opulent living was enjoyed for over a century, but then, with the evolution of history, that mode of living declined and the family abandoned the house. The building luckily escaped the Great House torching of the Troubles and survived to tell the tale. It was bought in 1928 for £10,000 by the Patrician Brothers, who ran it as a boarding school until the beginning of this century. It was during this period that I had first heard of it. But despite all the efforts of the Brothers, the maintenance of such an enormous building was far beyond their meagre resources and the structure continued to decline, until eventually part of the roof collapsed and the Brothers were forced to abandon it. At this point there were rumblings that the State might buy it for preservation purposes, but that never happened. Then in 2002 knights in shining armour came over the horizon: a wealthy American couple, Fred and Kay Krehbiel (she is Irish), undertook its restoration. And so the dream began.

To effect any major restoration requires not only hard cash, but also vision, precision and a dream. Here in Innishannon we had seen such a dream realised, admittedly on a much smaller scale because Cor Castle is far smaller than Ballyfin, but still a major undertaking. Cor Castle was a complete ruin because, unlike Ballyfin, it had not escaped the burnings of the Troubles. Trees were growing up through it and the windows and doors were gaping holes, and it seemed destined to remain just another ruined Irish house. But the grandson of the house had a dream that one day he would restore it and he did just that. It took time and probably a lot of money, but now it is a stunningly restored, comfortable family home. It is wonderful to see the past and present blended together for the enrichment of the future.

That night on TV I watched the carefully recorded restoration of Ballyfin. It was fantastic that the whole restoration was so well-documented. It began with the rebuilding of the giant conservatory that was linked to the main house. This wrought-iron, curvilinear Victorian conservatory was designed in 1855 by Richard Turner, one of the most important glass-house designers of his day, but in later years had deteriorated into a tangle of sagging iron roof and shattered glass. But all that was about to be transformed. A new creation was about to take place.

It was spellbinding to observe the huge, domed glass panels of the new conservatory roof being slipped carefully into place. This was an enormous job that had to be undertaken with the delicacy and precision of moving butterfly wings. One slip and all was lost. I sighed with relief when it was achieved and the completed conservatory stood sparkling in the sun. The first phase of the dream had been realised.

Then the challenging task of the house restoration began and it made for impressive viewing. But in the midst of this gigantic undertaking one happening became imprinted on my mind, one poignant detail that stood out above all others. It was the fact that during the decline of the house, when it was still a boarding school and in the care of the Patrician Brothers, one Brother had lovingly collected some of the beautiful old floor panels that were about to deteriorate beyond redemption. What visionary foresight from a man who obviously loved the place and must have watched in despair as it crumbled, though he was helpless to prevent it. But some instinct must have fanned a belief that one day a restoration would take place. He was preserving the flame and handing on the torch of restoration, enabling those who came after him to do what was beyond his capabilities. Wouldn't you love to salute this gallant, unsung hero! I hope that his spirit is now enjoying the restored Ballyfin.

Another scene that stayed with me from that viewing was the blending of the decor of Lady Coote's boudoir to harmonise with the lake view from the window. Unlike that Patrician Brother, Lady Coote probably took her opulent surroundings for granted, nevertheless she was to become part of the story that is Ballyfin.

The meticulous detail and precision of planning that went into the entire restoration was impressive. Local craftspeople were brought on board and all their old skills resurrected, and others sourced from around the world. Old paintings and family portraits that were scattered worldwide in various galleries were brought back. It was wonderful to watch it all unfold. On completion, Ballyfin has become a very exclusive top-class hotel, which may never pay for its restoration.

When the programme was over I decided that one day I would visit Ballyfin. I was not sure how this would happen, but there and then decided that it would. It went on my bucket list. A few months later, the programme was repeated on another channel and I watched it again, and was even more impressed the second time around. Soon after, I was up the country doing a reading and on the way home decided to make a detour and drive by Ballyfin. I stood outside the locked gate and had my photo taken. Next step was to get inside that gate! The dream was still alive.

On the wall of my attic where I retreat to write I have posted a little message: 'Hold fast to dreams for if dreams die life is a broken-winged bird that cannot fly.' But sometimes you have to put wings under dreams. So I decided to try to put a little flutter beneath the wing of my Ballyfin dream.

This year, on the last day of February, I had a big birthday, so without breathing a word to anybody I decided that I would write to Ballyfin and request a special favour of a visit by a non-resident – maybe for lunch, dinner or afternoon tea. Back came a courteous reply saying that in order to preserve the privacy of their residents they were not open to non-residents. I had told nobody that I had written that letter, and neither did I tell them about the reply. For some reason that I could not quite explain, I had kept a copy of the letter and now I put the reply into the same envelope and hid it in my desk. It was as if I was slightly embarrassed by my longing to see Ballyfin.

So, for my birthday I decided that instead of Ballyfin I would settle for a visit to St Mel's Cathedral in Longford to see their beautiful restoration, as St Mel's requires no prior arrangements and was open to all comers. But I decided to put that visit on hold for sunnier days when the journey would be more enjoyable.

And, by a strange coincidence, the day of my birthday, on which I had had my secret grand plan of travelling to Ballyfin, the whole country was on lock-down, holding its breath, waiting for the arrival of Storm Emma and the big freeze-up. So if I had been on the road to Ballyfin I could have been holed up in a giant snowdrift in the Slieve Bloom Mountains for days. It was a case of 'be careful of what you wish for, you might get it.'

But on the Saturday before my birthday and the big freeze, my niece Eileen and I went on a shopping spree to our favourite boutique in Bandon. Eileen had rung me during the week to say that the spring range was coming in and that maybe this would be a good time to see what they had. Eileen and I have different approaches to shopping. While I will quickly flick along the rails concentrating on my favourite colours, Eileen will meticulously work her way through every garment and will sometimes come upon something that I might have flicked past. And when she swung a lovely cream dress with a flush of red roses along its skirt off the rail, I immediately declared, 'That's my Garden and Galleries outfit!' Gardens and Galleries is a celebration that we have in Innishannon in summer when several gardens and art galleries open up to the public. It is a big occasion for us when we all put our best foot forward and aim to look good.

So now I had an outfit for the occasion.

Usually when Eileen and I go shopping, we make a day of it, but on this occasion I had to be home to babysit as my daughter, Lena, had told me that she had a meeting and her husband, Vincent, a GAA training session. So Eileen dropped me off outside their door and I headed in to do the needful. But when I opened the front door I was met by an eerie silence, which was unusual as the two small ones were usually making a racket. So, slightly alarmed, I ran down the hall and whipped open their kitchen door. I was absolutely flabbergasted to be faced by the entire extended family singing 'Happy Birthday'. The whole tribe had gathered while I was out shopping. It was a bolt from the blue. I was stunned. But we had great fun.

Later that evening a heavy, flat parcel was placed in front of me on a low table. I opened it carefully and was thrilled to discover a large photo album of family pictures from years back, which Lena had gathered from the entire tribe. For months previously, while I was babysitting and she and her husband were supposedly gone to meetings or training sessions, they were actually holed up in my attic scanning old photos. We were always a camera-happy family. My brother, Tim, had a camera when we were all very young, and my twenty-first birthday present from my sister, Phil, was an old Brownie camera. So, apart from my albums, this new album held photos of other family members going away back to childhood and up to the present day. We had great fun remembering the different events and occasions long gone.

Then, at the very back of the album, I came on the photo of myself taken the previous year outside the gates of Ballyfin, and beneath it written: 'Alice outside Ballyfin.' Beside it was a blank photo space and beneath that was written: 'Alice enjoying her Birthday Present of a trip to Ballyfin.'

The dream had come true. Ballyfin – here I come!

Sisters

Whoever thought of them first,
What a great idea!
At times we may not always think so,
When you feel like dumping one or two in the
well or dumping them in the tank!
All in all I think sisters were a wonderful idea,
especially if they were as wonderful and as kind
or contrary as mine
We have been together now for so years,
sharing, caring, arguing, learning,
agreeing, and are still sisters
I change anything,
...self and keep refl...
... read
...he bend

Alice outside Ballyfin

(Ballyf...
picture to b...
Happy Birthd...

Alice enjoying...
Birthday Present of...
to Ballyfin...

The Year of the
Big Snow

We were well warned. The previous week Met Éireann had told us in no uncertain terms that it was coming. They had been alerted by their outlying weather stations and had relayed the alarming forecast to us. Two serious weather warriors were heading in our direction. The Met service was sending out advance alerts and giving us ample warning to sit up and take notice.

Then on the Monday they began to issue more dire warnings that these two weather warriors were approaching from two different angles. The Beast from the East was stealthily bearing in upon the south east of the country while Storm Emma was raging up towards the south. The Beast, which would be first to arrive, was going to smother us under mountains of snow, and Storm Emma, coming in on top of her, was hell-bent on taking control and belting her in all directions. They were going to tear into each other and fight it out on top of us. We would be the battlefield.

Met Éireann made it sound ominous. We wondered if it could possibly be as bad as they were forecasting. Could they be exaggerating? Could it possibly be that brutal? But then we remembered Hurricane Ophelia the previous October and recalled that they had been spot-on about her. They had earned our respect. Dire weather warnings had preceded Ophelia – and then, too, we had wondered were they exaggerating? But, boys oh boys, were they right! Ophelia was short, sharp and deadly. She tore through the country, ripping roofs off buildings, tearing ancient trees from their deep roots, plunging the country into darkness and leaving three people dead. She left behind a trail of destruction and devastation.

While she raged, I had watched from inside my front window as she ripped sheets of galvanised roofing off a shed across the road and swirled them into the air. I then retreated and looked out the back window into the garden, where, to my consternation, the trees were bent to the ground before her brutal force. It was scary stuff!

Met Éireann could be right this time as well, so it was better to take no chances. If we were caught unprepared we would only have ourselves to blame. So we got ready. The Met office told us to batten down the hatches and we did just that, having first gathered in our nuts like squirrels preparing for winter. But instead of nuts, it was bread that we gathered to our bosoms. The shops were emptied of bread and milk. Schools closed, public transport was cancelled and the country waited with bated breath.

Ahead of the battle the temperature dropped. Then on Wednesday, 28 February, which was my birthday, the Beast from the East nosed in stealthily, sending cold shivers down our spines, and quietly began to take over. The Beast took a new avenue of approach into Ireland, and because she came in from the east the high hills of Kerry and the west coast were at first unaware of her presence – normally they would be the first to come under snow cover – so down here we began to wonder what all the fuss was about. But it was only a temporary respite. The Beast would get around to them once she had dealt with the south east and the midlands.

Met Éireann warned that 4pm on Thursday, 1 March, was the deadline when the Beast would really begin to assert her authority over us, then Storm Emma would rage in and batter us into subjection. During this battle it would be best to withdraw indoors and stay put until Met Éireann told us it was safe to emerge. Evelyn Cusack and Gerry Murphy, with their band of wise weather women, became our foster parents. In different circumstances they could have been directing elections – not alone were they issuing weather warnings, but forecasts dominated every main news bulletin and we had all-day weather updates, with experts and government ministers keeping us informed. So we did as we were told. Well … most of us did. But there will always be a few to challenge the warnings and drag out the emergency services to rescue them. But they were very few. The country on the whole had enough cop-on to stay home and enough food stashed to sustain us through a famine.

And then the weather unfolded exactly as predicted. There is an old adage that if March comes in like a lion, she will go out like a lamb. This year she certainly came in like a lion, a white lion. She prowled around the south east and south and smothered us in deep snowdrifts, but later got around to all the other areas of the country, where she also left her mark. And then Storm Emma raged in and took her on. The two of them brought down electric wires and froze water pipes, plunging many regions into chaos and crippling medical help. Hospital personnel made Trojan efforts to maintain emergency services, and many in the public service worked far above and beyond the call of duty to rescue and care for vulnerable people. With runways buried in snow and ice, flights were grounded. The weather brought mayhem to the farming world where tormented cows bellowed for water and demanded to be milked. But the milking machines would not work and the water taps were frozen solid. Neighbours came to each other's rescue and heroic people worked wonders in the prevailing conditions. When challenged by the two weather warriors, Ireland showed backbone and stamina, and we once again discovered the value of good neighbours and decent, dependable people.

Here in Innishannon, as all over Ireland, we awoke on that Friday morning to a quiet, white, silent world. As the road through Innishannon is the main artery into West Cork, on any normal day 30,000 vehicles pass through. We live with the constant sound of non-stop traffic. Every morning when I wake up, before opening my eyes I can gauge the time by the sound of the traffic. But on that morning not a purr of an engine was to be heard. There was absolute silence. When I opened my front door, which is on the village corner, I walked out into a deserted world. Standing in the middle of the village crossroads and looking west to Bandon, east to Cork and north to Macroom, not a car or human being was in sight. It was a deserted village, a rare moment when, like Alexander Selkirk, I was 'monarch of all I surveyed'. The trees along the street were transformed into giant Christmas trees and above the snow-laden roofs our two elegant church steeples were etched against the skyline. On the hill above the village, Dromkeen Wood was covered in soft, white duvets of snow. The village looked picture-postcard beautiful. It was a rare and truly amazing sight.

Then I trudged through the snow down towards the eastern end of the village to take a photograph of our 'Horse and Rider' sculpture at the Cork entrance. Progress was slow as the snow was soft and fluffy, which meant that you sank well down into it as you moved along. From sheer force of habit, I was walking on the footpath, and then Tadhg, our local guard, came out of the barracks and advised, 'Walk in the middle of the road, Alice, as that snow could come off the roof in big sheets and cover you.' It seemed strange to be walking out in the middle of the main road where normally without the permission of the green man you would not dare place a foot. The snow had certainly changed our perspective. Storm Emma had skirted by the village, though on the higher areas around us it had crippled the farming world.

Later in the day people began to emerge from their houses onto the street and come down from the estates up the hill to survey the now deserted village, many taking photograph of this rare sight. People were delighted to meet and greet after the lockdown. Children brought out makeshift sleighs and slid down the hills. Snowmen began to appear in the most unlikely places. The village took on a carnival atmosphere. We were all delighted to link up again and enjoy our empty village, which we knew would not last too long. By evening, the cars were beginning to crawl in and normality was returning.

On our village walkabout we talked about the last freeze-up of 2009, and the one in 1982, and further back to 1962. But there was no one to recall the big snow of 1947, only myself. Anyone who lived through that year forever afterwards referred to it as the 'Year of the Big Snow'. And it certainly was that. Because that year, from January to March, it snowed and snowed and snowed. A freezing blizzard created huge snowdrifts everywhere.

I was eight years old, becoming nine, in the middle of that big snow. Sometime after Christmas of 1947 and before my ninth birthday, I got my first pair of wellington boots. I was over the moon. These were a major step forward in a child's life. In my innocence I thought that wellingtons would not let the snow in no matter how deep the drift. I got a big shock on jumping into a deep snow drift when both my wellingtons filled up with snow that quickly turned to cold slush.

Our house and the surrounding countryside was smothered in deep snowdrifts that did not melt for weeks and weeks. We could walk around the fields and out over the gates and ditches that were turned into snow-mountains. If, during the day, the snow melted slightly, it froze again at night and snowed over again and again. There was no reprieve. To us children it was wonderful, and we built snowmen and pelted each other with snowballs. But for the adults it must have been quite another story, though, looking back now I realise that we were in many ways very self-sufficient. We were very far from a town but all we needed from the outside world was a packet of candles and a gallon of paraffin oil — and for my father, of course, who would have had withdrawal symptoms without it, batteries for the radio. At that time the radio ran on two heavy glass batteries, one of which was a wet battery that had to be charged occasionally in the local town. The dry battery was a long-distance runner, but the wet one was thirsty and had a melt-down into silence without its regular fix. That fix, strangely enough, in our town was provided in the local pub. So someone had to drag the bloody battery, which was very heavy, into town to keep my father in touch with the outside world, which he thought might grind to a halt if he was out of orbit. Other than these necessities, we were pretty self-sufficient. We had our own milk, as one or two cows were kept milking over winter to provide the household with the needful. The others were heavy with calf and happy to lie in their stalls where hay was drawn to them every morning, and they were let out later to the spout where water flowed down from the Glen further up the land. After the Christmas markets, animal numbers were much reduced on the farm, so it was just a case of keeping those who remained fed and watered. The hens alone had huge objections to the snow and cackled in alarm when their door was opened in the morning. They adamantly refused to venture out. To them, this white world outside their house was an alien country and they wanted nothing to do with it. But they kept us supplied with sufficient eggs, though not a large amount because the cold did affect their production. Ample food was available for all the animals as the grain was stored up in the loft and the barn was full of hay.

In the kitchen my mother baked daily, which was the norm in all households, drawing flour from the two drums containing white and brown flour that had been brought from the mill where our own wheat was milled, and now stored by the fire to keep it dry. In a barrel in the room off the kitchen, salted bacon from the pig killed in the autumn kept hunger at bay. Potatoes and turnips were stored in a pit behind the house. At that time if you were living deep in the country, an essential pre-Christmas purchase was a chest of tea; the only coffee available was a brand called Irel, and that was an acquired taste and not favoured by us children. Milk was consumed in many ways: big tin 'ponnies' of warm milk, and 'goody', which was bread soaked in milk with a generous sprinkling of sugar and was a great comforter – and, of course, cocoa was a favourite nighttime beverage. The cold, which penetrated every corner of the house, was the main problem during the Big Snow and I remember wearing our outdoor coats in the house. Clothes at the time were mostly made of warm wool, jumpers were handknit, and covering us in the beds at night were heavy twill sheets, wool blankets and large, heavy, homemade quilts. The main source of heat in the house was the large open fire in the kitchen, for which turf was stored in a reek out in the yard and in the turf house, and was constantly being drawn in. Logs from fallen trees were stacked in huge heaps at the end of the house. An old neighbour who used to trudge across the fields to us would say, 'This is no weather for sparing turf,' and how right she was. Neighbours kept in touch and young ones were dispatched around to old neighbours to make sure that all was well – my mother always sent us out in pairs and now I realise that she was afraid of us getting buried in the snowdrifts.

For the adults it must have been tough and I remember my uncle, who lived further back the valley with my grandmother, coming on horseback to let my mother know that all was well with Nana and to make sure that all was well with us.

But to us children it was simply great fun. And no school! The delight of being free all day every day to enjoy this glorious white wonderland was intoxicating. We were free to make wobbly sleighs and to slide down slippery slopes, and when the snowballing and snowman-building was done, our daily chore was feeding the birds. We scattered breadcrumbs over the snow outside the kitchen window and then stood inside and watched them swoop down to polish them off. My father, who knew the names of most birds, introduced us to the different types and, though he was not usually into drawing, he drew sketches of them in an old school copybook. With the farm buried in snow the work had shrunk, and there was time for him to do other things.

That was 1947, which in later years became known as the Year of the Big Snow. One wonders by what term will the snow of 2018 be remembered?

A Little Bit of
Heaven

My grandmother made bread-and-butter pudding to use up her stale bread leftovers and eating it was a test of endurance. But the bread-pudding in Kelly's of Rosslare is a sumptuous tempta-tion and a delight to the palate. I had almost convinced myself not to follow my healthy lunch of mouth-watering salmon salad with a dessert. But faced with a dish overflowing with gorgeous plump fruit thatched with fluffy layers of golden brown crust, my resolve melted. To further break down my resistance, beside the dish was a large bowl of freshly whipped cream, begging to be spooned. Irresistible! Having filled my bowl with feather-light pudding and layered it with an eiderdown of cream, I withdrew to a sunlit corner to sit back into a body-comforting Queen Anne arm-chair, savour my delight and observe my surroundings. Around me, but at a pleasant, non-intrusive distance, floated people of all ages, including toddlers with their

parents. The amazing feat of Kelly's is that they successfully combine catering for three generations, and none impinges on another. The seniors here were the well-heeled and comfortably retired, now enjoying the results of their labours, and then there were the high-earning young couples, both working fulltime and exhausted from rushing between the deadlines of crèches and high-pressure jobs; now they were having a much-needed break to recover their equilibrium. Their children were extraordinarily well behaved, I noticed, which made me recall a book that I had picked up for my daughter in a bookshop in Temple Bar in Dublin a few years previously: *French Children Don't Throw Food*, by Pamela Druckerman. It was wittily written by an American mother who moved with her child to Paris and was very impressed by the behaviour of the French children, especially when dining out in restaurants. The parents in Kelly's must all have read that book! In the case of some of the families, three generations were here together. Then there were some mothers and daughters having a relationship reunion, and members of bridge and other clubs having time away together, and women in small groups enjoying the good life. And around all these, Kelly's have created a luxury home-from-home experience, with gourmet food and wraparound comfort that is maintained at an immaculate level of perfection by a well-coordinated, pleasant staff, who constantly and unobtrusively pick up and remove. As soon as you no longer need it, it is gone, and as soon as you need a replacement it is there.

This year I came to Kelly's for the first time for a spring treat at the invitation of my daughter and son-in-law, who have two small children. They were taking a well-earned break from that breakneck routine that seems to be the norm for all young couples trying to balance the demands of jobs and children.

On the way there, five-year-old Ellie exuded anticipation. She had been there the previous year and was a Kelly enthusiast. To her, Kelly's was as near to heaven as she could get. She forecast, with a beaming smile, 'Nana, you will love Kelly's.' I was full of curiosity. Over the years, of course, I had heard of Kelly's. Who hasn't! But I had no idea what made it so special. All I knew was that there seemed to be a general consensus abroad that once you had been to Kelly's you became a patron for life. For this very reason I had occasionally wondered what it was all about. And now I was about to find out.

You arrive at Kelly's almost unaware that you are there. It is located on the side of the street with an across-the-road carpark, so there is no long-distance view to size up your surroundings, no long, winding avenue with an imposing mansion in the distance. There is no big impressive entrance. You simply slip into a long hallway, the top of which serves as the reception area, where friendly, smiling staff give you the impression that they are absolutely delighted to see you. Down along one side of this glass-fronted, long entrance hall are narrow tables with comfortable benches overflowing with plump cushions, and everywhere flowers and plants. Upright, elegant orchids interlink along the table-tops.

As we entered I noticed an elderly man relaxing in an ample armchair, his glasses precariously balanced on the end of his nose, snoring gently with an abandoned book on his knees. My daughter smiled knowingly in his direction and said, 'We've arrived.' You somehow get the feeling that you have come into a comfortable family home rather than into a grand hotel. The immediate impression is of brightness, relaxation and welcome.

My extended family was directed to a large room on the ground floor containing a double bed, two single beds and a cot, with double doors opening on to an inviting lawn. Everything was white, bright and immaculate. Ellie picked her bed and settled in like a swallow returning to its nest. She was looking forward to the pool, the kiddies' disco, the play area and the sandcastles.

I was located on the floor above, with every conceivable comfort to keep me happy, and once settled in I picked up a little brochure of hotel activities. To my absolute amazement and delight I discovered that the well-known TV gardener Dermot O'Neill would be giving a two-hour talk the following morning, and for the further two mornings. What a bonus! Talk about having jam and jam up on it! I am no gardening expert, but I am an avid learner, and there is no end to learning on the garden trail. Because I was a late-comer to the joys of gardening, I am forever trying to catch up. So the prospect of listening to an expert like Dermot O'Neill for three mornings was like manna from heaven. I was tickled pink! My three days were off to a flying start.

Later, the children had a disco where they danced, pranced and chased each other around the little sectioned-off area of the dance floor in the Ivy Room, and then were served dinner, after which they went to an adjacent play area where they were looked after by smiling, cheerful staff while parents could have a relaxed dinner in comfort. Children are not allowed into the main dining room, called The Beaches, for dinner, which gives adults a chance to enjoy a child-free zone. Guests dress up for dinner and the atmosphere in the dining room is formal and elegant, which is fitting for the gourmet food served. Leaving the dining room you feel as if you have been out for dinner in a posh restaurant. If the children got restless, the staff had no problem serving parents their dessert in another room where they could join their children. After dinner a band played music in the Ivy Room, which was then also out of bounds to children so that adults could enjoy dancing and the use of the nearby bar.

On retiring, I discovered that my bed was a 'please do not leave me' bed, and the bedroom chairs were ideal for reading or writing. Breakfast was served in The Beaches or you could help yourself in the Ivy Room where the self-service choice was unbelievable. Ellie had a great time making her own pancakes on a little magic machine that knew exactly what to do once she pressed the right buttons.

Afterwards, on sauntering around the hotel, I discovered comfortable armchairs in every corner and an arresting array of paintings on the walls. A collection of photos along one corridor brought a smile to my face. Amongst them was a photo of two sunny-faced nuns whose faces portrayed the joys of life. They made you feel uplifted. Later I met a woman who told me that one of the nuns was her aunt and had spent all her life in the Benedictine Kylemore Abbey in Connemara. That nun's face told the story of a happy, deeply spiritual life.

Opening off another corridor was a large, comfortable room where a glowing fire was surrounded by armchairs inviting you to come in and read. Next a TV room, temporarily converted into a lecture hall, where a large contingent had gathered to listen to Dermot O'Neill. I was delighted to join them and for two hours Dermot poured forth pearls of gardening wisdom. It was extremely enjoyable and informative, and the questions afterwards revealed a high level of gardening expertise in the room.

Then lunch, which you could have served up to you in The Beaches restaurant or enjoy a trawl along the self-service tables of delights in the Ivy Room. Either way, an exquisite experience. Afterwards, a stroll around the imaginative garden of humps and hollows, incorporating a sunken tennis court and a series of hidden bridges, and sheltered, sea-facing rest areas. Sculptures along the way provided pleasant dawdling moments. Then down on to the beach where the variety of sea shells has to be seen to be believed. After an invigorating walk along the beach you could retire to the spa and spoil yourself with a choice of massages to soothe yourself into a state of total relaxation. If you were so inclined, afternoon tea was served at 4pm in the Ivy Room. The only problem with Kelly's is that were you to partake of all the meals available you would certainly go home with what is humorously referred to as a 'Kelly Belly'.

This hotel has been run by the Kelly family for

over a century and in that time they have fine-tuned their establishment to the highest level of effortless expertise. The strong team of well-coordinated, efficient staff keep the wheels turning with what appears to be seamless ease.

I left with the conviction that I too would be back. As Ellie had predicted, I had fallen in love with Kelly's.

Why Be Bothered?

Many years ago I walked the road from Bandon to Innishannon. When I reached the old bridge at Innishannon I stepped up into the little stone recess to avoid the rare vehicle that passed by and leaned in over the warm stones of the bridge to admire the scene below. It was a lovely sunny afternoon and the breathtaking view of the river flowing through the wooded Bandon valley on its way to Kinsale was wonderful. On one side of the river the hillside trees in Dromkeen Wood were just beginning to don their spring coats and on the other side the large green field along the bank of the river sloped gently up to the village where two elegant church spires towered above the trees. Further down along the river an old, grey ruined tower elbowed out above the water where two swans glided along. It was the most enchanting place that I had ever seen. I was just twenty years old – and three years later I came to live in Innishannon when I married the love of my life, who thought that Innishannon was the Promised Land.

Living next door to us were his Aunty Peg and Uncle Jacky. Jacky ran around the village every morning delivering papers and he did jobs for any elderly people living on their own. And every morning he brushed the street outside his shop, as did all the householders along the street. There was not much litter as there were no plastic bags, no cartons, and all milk and soft drinks were sold in returnable glass bottles. At that time, Aunty Peg was probably in her mid-fifties, and I thought that she was ancient!

Over the years I got absorbed into village life, though at the beginning I often resented my husband's dedication to his community. But he carried on regardless, and gradually I became a convert. He was on every committee in the village and gave unstintingly of his time. To him it was all about the community and the common good. As a teenager he had delivered telegrams on his bike all around the parish, so he knew every nook and cranny and back road of the place. From behind the post office counter, he gave out the Children's Allowance and Old Age Pension, so he knew everybody and everybody knew him. When I arrived on the scene I was the subject of much scrutiny to see if I was up to scratch, and one friend of Aunty Peg's told her, 'That wan won't do at all, sure there isn't a bit of her there!'

Eventually I almost became one of them, but

because my family had not been here for several generations I could still be perceived as a blow-in. But I
had no problem with that. Blow-ins can be very good
for a community and over the years I have seen many
newcomers give a sense of vibrancy and energy to
this place: people who are happy to do things for the
satisfaction it offers and for the improvement of their
surroundings.

As Innishannon changed from a quiet rural village
where we all knew each other to a village throbbing
with passing traffic, and as new housing estates were
built we became conscious that an effort was needed
to preserve the village ethos. It would be so easy to
evolve into a soulless collection of people who all
lived behind their own doors and did nothing to
enhance their community. People who come to live
in a community and decide to remain inside their
own doors and be non-productive members lose out
in the long run.

Even though organisations and voluntary efforts
can at times annoy the living daylights out of you and
meetings can be drawn-out exercises of mental torture,
there eventually comes a time when a breakthrough
is made, and with it comes a thrill of great satisfaction
and a sense of euphoria that something that has taken
years of effort to achieve finally gets conquered, and
the entire community breathes a sigh of satisfaction.

There is great therapy in that doing and achieving. Intellectual knowledge is not the same thing as truly understanding things from the centre of your being, which results from experiencing and doing.

Where we live has a huge influence on our sense of wellbeing and if we allow ourselves to be surrounded by litter and disorder, we soon begin to feel bad. I recall going into a particular housing estate in a nearby town one time. It was full of litter and was a depressing sight. To wake up there every morning and come home to it every night could not be good for the wellbeing of the people living there. We had that problem in a housing estate here too, but two great women living there transformed it and it is now a beautiful place.

The different ways that we view our community is always fascinating and in every place we can have three different streams of thinking: the 'they', the 'ye' and the 'we'. The first lot demand: 'Why don't they do it?' 'They' could either be the government, the council or any other nameless body. Then we have the 'Why don't ye do it?' brigade. People who see voluntary organisations like Tidy Towns, the GAA, the Parish Hall Committee or any voluntary group as a vehicle to do things they think should be done, but have no notion of doing themselves.

But don't you love people who say, 'We will do it.'

These are the lifeblood of every community. They see things that need to be done and help get them done. These people are happy to do things for their own satisfaction and the improvement of their surroundings. Theirs is the realisation of achievement for its own sake and they are not dependent on the appreciation or criticism of others. For them the satisfaction lies in a job well done.

Voluntary organisations all over the country are held together by these people and they are the lifeblood of every community. They never think: 'Why be bothered?'

Our Bee Garden

Every year we mean to have our Tidy Towns AGM early and every year it simply doesn't happen. A multitude of reasons always seems to crop up for putting it on the long finger. But maybe the real reason behind this delaying tactic is that we all know that once we hold our AGM we are down to the grindstone of the weekly work nights – brushing, washing, painting, digging and planting. All voluntary hard graft. You simply cannot put a gloss on the fact that Tidy Towns is based on the slave-labour principle. But unlike the slavery of old, when the taskmaster was a man with a whip, the Tidy Towns taskmaster is a dream, but a dream that drives us on as relentlessly as any man with a whip. That dream is founded on love of place, and like any doting parent who believes that their progeny has the possibility to be the best, so it is with Tidy Towners. Proud homeowners want their house to look good, but Tidy Towners go a step further, out their own front door, along the street and along approach roads. It's a walk out into the larger

communal home of the family to which we belong. The plus side of Tidy Towns is the common bond of togetherness and the satisfaction of communal achievement. To quote the late and gifted journalist Con Houlihan, who had a great sense of place, it is all 'for the sake of the little place'.

So this year, when Margaret Griffin of Griffin's Garden Centre sent out a notice in April of an information day for Tidy Towns groups on how best to achieve their potential, we, of course, answered her call. Apart from Margaret's talk, which we knew would be inspirational, a meeting and pooling with other Tidy Towns enthusiasts is always a learning curve. It had been a long, long winter of storms, snow and non-stop rain. We all needed stimulation and motivation to recover and to get going. A day in the sun was what we all needed. And the sun obliged.

When we arrived, Margaret's garden centre was vibrant with people and colour. We caught the tail-end of the previous talk, which was drawing to a close with the planting of a tree. We wandered around the garden centre marvelling at the colour coordinations and the different mini gardens on display. Then it was time for our afternoon session and we trooped into a large garden shed so skillfully blended into the surrounding trees that it was almost invisible.

Margaret began her talk on how approach roads

tell the story of their place as one of the key elements that the Tidy Towns judges are looking for, and she showed slides of places that met the required criteria. When Innishannon came up on screen as a village that told its story well to anyone driving through, we were pleasantly surprised. This plaudit was due entirely to the sculptures of the 'Horse and Rider' and the 'Blacksmith' at either end of the village, which between them tell the story of the origins of our village.

But the project that really captured our imaginations this year was the idea of creating a bee garden in the village to help preserve and sustain our bee life. As we are all well aware, bee life is threatened as the result of our detrimental treatment of the environment, and if anything should happen to the bees we won't be long after them. We need their pollinating power to sustain our food chain.

So we decided to do our bit for the bees and we had the ideal location ready and waiting. Well, waiting if not exactly ready! At the western side of our parish hall is a sheltered, sloping area facing south, which had previously been the home of a giant Leylandia that had outlived its welcome and had recently been removed. Now this sunny corner was available. It was the perfect location for our bee garden.

First on the agenda was a visit to the local garden centre run by Willie Granger, who was on our wavelength about bee-loving plants. As we walked around his centre, Willie introduced us to his selection of suitable plants and we estimated that we would need over a hundred plants for our designated area. This was Saturday, and we planned to plant on Monday, so we let it to Willie to work on our plant requirements over the weekend.

Come Monday, a tight strimming of the area by our two FÁS workers, known affectionately as the 'Two Johns', took place. FÁS is a wonderful scheme whereby workers provide assistance to voluntary groups three days a week and then they can do other jobs for the remaining two days. We are blessed with our Two Johns. When the strimming was completed we went to collect our plants.

Willie had them lined up on trolleys ready for collection. Back at base, careful placing took time, and then came the 'big dig'! Let's say that the ground was not soft, pliable and ready to receive the plants with open arms, so a long afternoon of tough digging began. While this was in progress, a young couple came along and admired the work in progress. 'Do you want help?' the husband enquired in a pronounced American accent.

I looked at him with wide-eyed delight. Any offer of help in Tidy Towns is gratefully received. Then I recognised him as one of the new people who had

turned up at our AGM and had also come the following work night. New volunteers for Tidy Towns
activities are a gift from the gods. Most people think
that Tidy Towns is a splendid organisation, but when
they discover that it basically involves hard labour their
ardour cools a little. But not Joshua, who, true to his
word, arrived back at the digging site – armed with
three teenage children! And these teenagers knew
how to apply themselves to the job on hand, and so
eventually the last plant was put in place.

Now, this was not going to be a tidy, well-disciplined
plot. That was not the idea. Bees and butterflies are not
into perfectly maintained gardens where order is the
name of the game. They need a space where nature has
a free run. This would probably cause comment about
a 'badly kept patch'. So to illustrate the point that this
was a garden for bees not humans, we decided that we
needed a beehive to proclaim that this was to be 'bee
territory'.

So, the search for a beehive got underway. No
working beekeeper would, understandably, part with
a beehive, so other avenues had to be explored. An
old-fashioned beehive with an apex roof would best
answer our requirements – they are somehow more
visually appealing than the modern, flat-roofed variety.

I had been reared with a beekeeping brother, so I
sent an enquiry back to the home farm from where

the beekeeper has now gone on to heavenly pastures, but, unfortunately, so had all his bee-keeping para- phernalia. So an SOS went out around the parish for the roof of a beehive. Once we had the right roof the rest of the hive could be made up. And the roof was found! Doris, whose late husband, Walter, had been a wonderful beekeeper, searched her garden shed and unearthed the perfect roof. The sight of it warmed my heart and brought back memories of rows of beehives under the trees in the grove behind our home when I was a child. The world of beekeeping is full of wonder and delights. There is something magical about going out late on a summer's evening to stand beside a hive and listen to the hum within. Or hiving a swarm that has left the old hive – you place them in front of a new hive and watch as the queen bee leads her army of workers towards the entrance to a their new home. Magical! But now, due to our love affair with weed- killers, our bee population is endangered and we need to look after them.

Our small bee and butterfly garden is only a tiny effort, but still worthwhile. We now had the roof of our hive, and one of our old reliables, Paddy, made the rest of it and then we painted it yellow and placed it in the middle of the garden. The whole area is filled with colours that the bees love – mostly blue, yellow and lilac, with some pink and orange and red. Later

in the summer, Jerry, one of our local artists, painted a matching mural of bees and sunflowers on the wall of the parish hall beside it. It brings a smile to the face of all who pass by.

A Scrape of Religion

As I came in from the garden the phone was ringing. A familiar voice at the other end saluted with 'Hi, Taylor', a title by which I am addressed by only one member of the family. It was my eldest, from whom a phone call is a rare and wonderful occurrence. This son is not into the social niceties of mother-and-son long, chatty phone calls. He might ring if the house was on fire, or if he had crashlanded on to a desert island – though maybe not even then, as he believes that what mother does not know will not bother her. So, a phone call out of the blue on a sunny summer's day was a bit of a bolt from the blue.

'Where are you?' I asked in amazement, thinking that he might have landed on Mars.

'Knock,' he announced.

'Knock?' I gasped in shock. If he had said Mars I would not have been more thunderstruck. 'What in the name of all's that good and holy are you doing

in Knock?' He is one of the present generation who has decided, like so many of his peers, that religion is now surplus to requirements. So to hear that he was in Knock was almost beyond belief.

'I am up here to meet a guy about a model truck and on the way to meet another man. As I was driving along the road I saw a signpost for Knock.'

'And …' I prompted, feeling the need to know more from this son who is not into the minute details so beloved of his mother.

'Well, I wasn't here since Dad brought us when I was about seven on a bus from Innishannon. And for some reason I remembered that just now when I saw the sign, so I turned the car and headed here.'

'Well, miracles do happen!' I breathed.

But before I got carried away with enthusiasm, he demanded, 'Do you want anything from Knock?'

I was too stunned to quickly summon my wits about me, and while I gathered my thoughts he announced, 'I rang you because you are the only one with a scrape of religion left in our crowd.'

'If you told me that you were in outer space I would not be more surprised,' I told him, but ignoring this he continued, 'I have walked the whole place and was delighted to see some of the old holy hurdy-gurdy shops still hanging in there. I went into the chapel and said a prayer of thanks that all is well.'

'Halleluia!' I proclaimed. 'Miracles do happen,' I repeated.

'Well, what do you want?' he demanded, before I got carried away on a cloud of false euphoria.

'A rosary beads,' I told him.

'Anything else?' he wanted to know.

'There is a very good bookshop there,' I told him, and asked him to look for two particular books.

'Will do,' he told me. 'See you later.' And that was that!

I sat down in the nearest chair, stunned. And, for some unexplainable reason, I was pleasantly surprised to get the call. It made me wonder about the strange twists and turns that beliefs take in our lives. On one of my earliest visits to Knock I had stood on the cold, bleak, windswept site where Monsignor Horan proposed to build his airport and had thought this man was either a lunatic or a visionary capable of working miracles. The fact that he succeeded was to me the first miracle at Knock.

Over the years, my husband Gabriel had been a regular visitor to Knock and had taken the children there at different ages. Obviously, some buried memories of the place had stayed with one of them and had been reawakened when he saw the signpost for Knock. That was my second miracle at Knock.

Voyage Complete!

I have arrived. My voyage is over. My six months' journey with the *Captain's Log* is complete. How was it? Challenging! The first few weeks out at sea were a bit stormy as I got my sail ropes entangled and I did not fill in my log book correctly. *Mea culpa!* This was due solely to the fact that I had not read the instructions properly. For some strange reason, I did not get the hang of the rules until a few weeks into the voyage. Then I re-read the instructions and got my sense of direction properly focused. A bit like any new undertaking, it took me a while to work out the rhythm and it was only by doing it that I mastered it. Sometimes I can be a bit of a slow learner. But finally I got it! Then, like Professor Higgins, I felt like singing, 'I got it, by George, I think I got it.' Finally, with all my ropes untangled, I was out to sea. My ship was in full sail. The voyage was underway. And the *Captain's Log* was to be the navigator.

The *Captain's Log* had to be filled in diligently every night. How did I find that? A bit of a commitment. After trying a few locations around the house in which to do the nightly write-up, I finally came to the conclusion that the kitchen table was the best port of call. Some nights I was halfway up the stairs to bed when I remembered the log and then had to come back down to do the needful, sometimes quietly swearing under my breath! Other nights, when I was very tired, I had to kick myself in order to sit down at the kitchen table to comply with the rules of the log and fill it in meticulously. There was no escaping this nightly discipline of the log routine. For some unexplainable reason, I felt that once I had begun I was on course, and I had to keep going. I could not abandon ship mid-voyage! I felt the need to give it a fair crack of the whip and was determined to keep up my commitment to the best of my ability.

The log book was divided into three sections and each section had its own bookmark. The monthly log section had a brown marker, the weekly log section had a cream marker and the daily section had a white marker. The entire log was laid out with military precision into months, weeks and days. I won't go into the details, but from this you get the idea: you had to plan ahead for the month, week and day, and make lists in order of priority. You then ticked off achievements, so you reviewed everything as you went along.

The real challenge for me was the daily log. Here

were three blank lines to be filled in with your Three Important Tasks for the following day and after them a space for Time Spent and a box for achievement or otherwise, to be filled that night. Beneath this came the encouragement: a wise quote from some ancient philosopher or sometimes a modern guru – always interesting, positive and encouraging.

'Luck is what happens when preparation meets opportunity,' Heraclitus.

'Wise men talk because they have something to say; fools because they have to say something,' Plato.

'Remembering that I will be dead soon is the most important tool I've ever encountered to help me make the big choices in life,' Steve Jobs.

'The unexamined life is not worth living,' Socrates.

Next came a gratitude section: 'Today I am grateful for ....' I had often heard of keeping a Gratitude Journal, but this was as near as I ever came to it. I was surprised by how much I had to be grateful for. Next came meditation, and you recorded the time spent.

The filling in of all this could be very interesting,

and made you stop and think back on your day.

Keeping the *Captain's Log* was a nightly chore, but it did organise my thinking and planning. It placed great emphasis on daily meditation and zoned you in on the need to make time to fit it in every day, which was a big challenge. Up to then I had make vague efforts in that direction, but there was nothing vague about the *Captain's Log*. Either you did it or you did not, and each night you had to answer to yourself. I found this a whole new experience because normally I function on impulse and a bit of a wing and a prayer. The *Captain's Log* forced me to get my act together and get things done that otherwise would have been put on the long finger.

When I finally reached port I felt a huge sense of achievement that I had stuck with it and made it to the end. It was a voyage I hadn't had to take, but once I read the *Captain's Log* I was overwhelmed by a deep sense of curiosity as to how it might work. Also, one could not but be impressed by the person who had planned and written it.

And it had proved to be a voyage well worth taking. It had deepened my sense of gratitude for little things and caused me to live more in the now.

Gardens and Galleries

Some people paint pictures on canvas with a brush or palette knife while others create pictures in a garden with a spade and a shovel. Both are drawing from their pool of creativity, bringing beauty into our world. In and around Innishannon we have many dedicated gardeners some of whom have formed a Flower and Garden Club where they love to share their gardening knowledge with each other. Some local artists have their own studios and also give classes, and many people enjoy painting under their watchful eye. Both activities are enriching for the creators themselves, and can be equally enriching when shared with other people.

So an idea was born. What if we created a showcase for these combined talents? A celebratory weekend for our local gardeners and artists? And so the idea for Gardens and Galleries emerged.

With any outdoor event in Ireland you are in the lap

of the gods where weather is concerned, and on this occasion we were going to be very weather dependent. Nobody enjoys traipsing around even the most beautiful garden beneath trees and shrubs dripping with rain, but on a sunny day it makes everybody feel good. Until this year we never had to worry about the weather being too hot!

The first hurdle to be overcome was to find out how many brave souls would be willing to open their garden gates and allow other gardeners in. Most people recoil in horror at the prospect, a very understandable reaction. A few years ago when faced with that request by a local fundraising group, I nearly fainted at the prospect of submitting my tangle of confusion to the gaze of knowledgeable gardeners. But one shrewd man, who knew a lot about the gardening world, advised, 'Your garden is grand and anyway all most people want is to get their nose inside someone else's garden gate.'

So I was persuaded, and every day for weeks afterwards regretted that decision. I berated myself for my weak-mindedness. Theirs was a worthy cause, but the cost in kneeling hours was enormous. Because once you decide to open your garden to the public you walk around it and view it through the eyes of a stranger. It puts you thinking! You see overgrown bushes beneath which sun-starved flowers are straining for light. You notice blousy shrubs that should have had manners put on them long ago. And so on it goes, all around the garden. I spent days weeding, with my head in the earth and my bottom up in the air. When weeding, you get to know every stone and worm in your soil. I began at the right-hand side of the garden gate and continued all the way around the garden, heading for the left-hand side. Finally I arrived there. By then I was crippled with exhaustion and fit only for the kitchen couch. But eventually I recovered.

My open day brought flocks of visitors, because, just as my advisor had told me, there is nothing that gardeners like better than visiting other people's gardens. It was a hugely enjoyable experience during which I met the most interesting people and learned quite a lot from gardeners who were far more knowledgeable about gardening than I was. It was a day full of surprises, worth all the effort – and my garden was perfect for the rest of the summer.

So now I had to convince other people of the joy of opening their gardens. I hoped that I would be as effective as my advisor had been. After much coaxing, cajoling, bribery (not corruption, but not far short of it!) we finished up with seven brave gardeners ready to open their gates. Amongst them we had a castle garden, a cottage garden, a village garden, a housing-estate garden, a farm garden and a riverside

garden. Needless to mention, the castle garden was the jewel in the crown, and what a jewel! It surrounds an old castle that the owner had inherited from his grandmother and had lovingly restored from a forlorn ruin into a beautiful, elegant home. Once the castle was restored he began on the gardens and was in the throes of bringing them back to their former glory. They were breathtaking! That garden was on the top of everybody's 'must see' list.

We had four artists ready to come on board and their students would also display their work in village venues. There was a big variety of paintings, as one artist is into portraiture, another flowers and another landscape. It was delightful to go from one gallery to another and view the different approaches and talk to the artists, and then into the group exhibitions where you met and chatted with their students.

The village households were encouraged to decorate their windows and we arranged a gramophone recital in a country market at one end of the village, and a display of vintage cars and artefacts in the forecourt of the garage in the centre of the village. Our two churches of different denominations were decorated by their members.

The action hub for the weekend was to be the Parish Hall at the western end of the village. Here people would receive a ticket and a map directing them to all the different venues. Some of the gardens were outside the village and people had the choice of driving around in their own car or hopping on the mini bus, generously provided by Rural Transport, and being driven around by local volounteers. But some visitors might enjoy simply walking along the village street. The proceeds would be ploughed back into the community – seats for the wood, window boxes for abandoned houses, new flower tubs for the village. As always with Tidy Towns, the list was endless, but top on our list of priorities was tree-planting. On a long slope between the Parish Hall and the bridge, many old trees had died. They needed to be removed and replaced by young native trees. Of all the activities we in Tidy Towns undertake, tree-planting is probably the most important.

Gardens and Galleries was well advertised – when running any event, getting the word out is the first vital step. Easier said than done! In today's world our brains are so battered with news and advertising belting at us from all angles that it is extremely difficult to be heard. So, making people aware that your event is worth visiting is a big challenge. But we tried hard and succeeded.

People began to arrive early into the village in large numbers. On the front wall of the Parish Hall we had a large map and standing beside it a knowledgeable local who could direct the visitors to their locations of choice. He was our 'Welcome-to-Innishannon Man'! People then set off with their own map. We had concentrated on excellent signposting so that strangers would not get confused and finish up somewhere other than where they intended going. All the plans had been well laid.

The event was a success beyond all our expectations. People loved it. They enjoyed going from garden to garden, and into the galleries where they met and chatted with old friends and neighbours, or indeed strangers. Open gardens invite conversation between strangers as gardening is the common denominator. People loved walking along the street, looking at the windows that home owners had dressed with great flair and variety. The little village café and our local hotel hummed with activity. Some people are big into the gardens, while for others it was all about the paintings. The display of vintage cars in the forecourt of Bernard Car Sales, hosted by Mick and Charlie, was crowded with men. It was obvious that this was a male-orientated hobby.

We were blessed with the weather as the sun shone brightly for the two days. The whole thing ran like clockwork. And the icing on the cake was that everybody had a smile on their face. Nothing brings out the best in people like viewing other people's creativity.

Gardening and painting are beautiful hobbies and the sharing of this creativity enriches both the artist and the viewer. It is food for the soul. By the end of the two days we were exhausted, but exhilarated.

The following morning I met Mick, who had master-minded the vintage car display, and he announced: 'Next year, now, we will do a much bigger vintage display.' His words brought joy to my heart. I loved his use of 'we' as opposed to 'ye' or 'they'! People who say 'we' are taking ownership of the undertaking and that is the key to the success of all community activities.

Too Hot to Handle

In mid-summer it hit us. Sizzled in on top of us. Before we knew what was happening we were being roasted alive. Nobody had warned us that it was coming. Back in January when the Big Freeze came Met Éireann were hoarse from giving us advance warning, but not a peep out of them about the hot-oven conditions that crashed in on top of us in June and July in 2018. We were sizzling on the spit before any red alert sounded.

A few weeks earlier the weather was so cold that there was no grass growth and the farmers worried that there would be no silage cut to feed the cattle. Then the cold eased and grass grew, but the country became shrouded in persistent rain and the farmers watched the forecast daily hoping to catch a few dry hours to cut the silage. They grasped any dry day. It literally was a case of 'making hay while the sun shines'. At that stage there was no indication that a heatwave, with sun-scorching, blazing days lay around the corner. And then, without warning, it swept in.

We were plunged from a cloying cloud of constant rain and drizzle into a blazing hot oven. Wow!

But did we complain? We were speechless with shock. This could not be happening in Ireland. And at first we were afraid to complain. We who constantly gripe and groan about our wet weather were afraid to moan when the sun scorched down and drained our energy. As we were melting in the heat of rising temperatures, we felt that we could not make a fuss lest we tempt our weather gods to turn on the usual taps and send us all back to square one with normal weather. So we shut up and scorched in silence. One honest man, however, whispered to me, 'I hate this bloody heat, but don't tell anyone I said that.'

But gradually our tolerance of the sweltering temperatures melted as the blazing conditions continued. It became permissible to give out. Green fields turned bronze, and, with no grass growth, farmers were forced to feed their cattle the silage stored for the forthcoming winter. Many young farmers, who had increased their herd numbers in recent years, came under extreme pressure. This was a whole new experience for Ireland. Usually it was the over-abundance of water that was our problem, but now the horror of dried up rivers and reservoirs loomed. For the first time in living memory, a countrywide water-hose ban was introduced – first in Dublin and then everywhere.

We became very water-use conscious and reused water for a multiplicity of purposes.

For the first time ever I turned off the Aga. I felt as if I was murdering my grandmother. The Aga is a constant presence in my life, and she cooks, heats, comforts and provides a permanent supply of hot water. But with soaring temperatures she was turning the large kitchen into an extension of her oven. So she had to bow out! Without her, I was bereft. An Aga is a friend for life and turning her off was like giving my best friend a slap in the face. It took two days for her to cool off and her water supply took a week to cool down. But gradually the kitchen became a shady retreat and I mastered the art of the microwave. Not an adequate replacement, but at least it kept hunger at bay.

The scorching days continued and we all tried to remember if we ever before had a summer like this. Anyone who remembered the Big Snow of 1947 recalled that it was followed by a scorching hot summer; my mother would have described those days as 'great days to wash blankets'. On the outer edges of my memory came back images of blankets and sheets strewn over hedges and heavy quilts spread out on grassy fields. And so I collected pillows and laid them out on bushes and draped washed bedspreads and blankets over hedges. Pillows came in at night engulfed with a heady garden aroma and that night the resulting sleep was deeper and more restful. The great outdoors had moved in. As temperatures forgot to come down from normal daytime to cooler night-time, we slept beneath sheets without blankets or duvets, and kept our windows wide open. Rumours of rain showers in other parts of the country floated past us, and we felt deprived. The weather forecasters gave little hope of a reprieve. We felt like slices of bread forgotten in a toaster. Beaches overflowed with sun worshippers and people abroad on sun holidays felt that they had wasted their money as we had the Costa del Sol at home.

Gardeners watched sadly as their favourite plants gave up the struggle and folded over, but we all felt that plants were of secondary importance to the priorities of animals and the farms. Here in Innishannon we were glad that Gardens and Galleries was behind us as no garden would be fit to open after weeks of this scorching, and even the tough hydrangeas along the approach roads to the village wilted and lost the battle to remain upright. Late at night I carefully watered my window boxes and hanging baskets along the street from a small jug of saved water.

Rain was forecast for the south on Thursday, 26 July, and we waited with bated breath. Would it come? Up to then we had only had a dribble here and there.

We were well over a month into this torrid heatwave. Surely rain would come? For the first time we could begin to understand what people in other countries have to endure when they need to walk miles for water, a scenario previously unimaginable in Ireland. The dilemma of farmers became the problem of all of us. With no rain there would be no crops, and animals could not survive without water. So we waited and hoped for rain. A lot of rain!

On the morning of the 26 July we woke up hoping to hear the patter of rain against the window, but silence reigned. I got out of bed and looked out over the garden. Not a drop of rain in sight, but a grey ominous sky looked promising. About 8am a slight drizzle came and then disappeared and the day blazed on, hot and clammy. But finally, at around 5pm, the rain came. A soft, misty, clammy rain that clung to parched trees and scorched grass. We hoped that it would continue for many hours. We felt like going out and dancing in it. Over the following days rain came spasmodically, but we needed lots of it. Lots and lots of it. For the first time that I can remember, rain had turned into holy water. We needed it to bless the land.

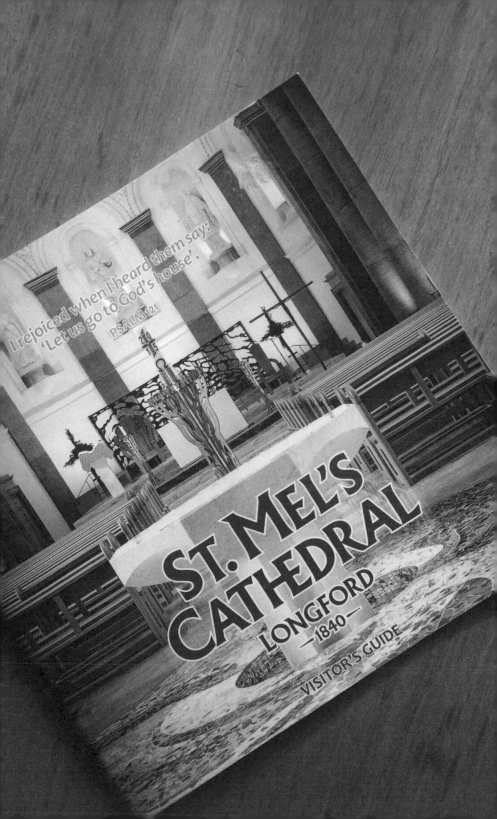

I rejoiced when I heard them say:
'Let us go to God's house'.
PSALM 121

ST. MEL'S CATHEDRAL

LONGFORD
—1840—

VISITOR'S GUIDE

We Will Rebuild

In the summer when the sweltering conditions had cooled a little and rain had at last come to moisten the parched earth, I made my way to St Mel's Cathedral in Longford. It's a long drive from Cork to Longford and on the way we passed a variety of signposts welcoming us to many counties of Ireland. But eventually Longford appeared on a signpost. As we drove towards the town, the dome of the cathedral rose majestically above all the other buildings. One felt that this town was focused around its cathedral.

Signs at the entrance to the town proclaimed Longford to be the 'cleanest town in Ireland', and with justification. The streets were spotless and made colourful by a profusion of flowers and well-maintained, brightly painted buildings. It was a fitting surrounding for their historic cathedral. One could not but be impressed.

When you push open the door into the main porch of St Mel's, you are immediately immersed in a huge photographic display of the burnt-out cathedral. It's an arresting introduction to the story that is about to unfold around you. And what a story!

It was Christmas night 2009 when St Mel's went up in flames. Overnight, this beautiful cathedral turned from a much-loved landmark building into a burning inferno that was devastated and desecrated by fire. Earlier that night it had been filled with joyful parishioners celebrating Christmas, but by morning their beautiful cathedral was a blackened ruin of smouldering wood, smashed stained-glass windows and blackened pillars. Next day I saw the devastation on the TV news and felt an ache of compassion and sympathy as I watched the stricken faces of the people for whom this had been their parish church, which had hosted all the significant happenings of their lives – their baptisms, weddings and funerals. Now it lay in ruins. The big question on everyone's mind must have been: How did this happen? Surely nobody did this deliberately? In such circumstances this question always comes to mind and casts an extra gloom over the situation. The thought that such a fire could have been ignited by the evil intent of arson would have made the calamity far more shocking. But, luckily, subsequent investigations were to prove otherwise and reveal that the fire had begun in an old chimney flue and spread to the sacristy. So it was just one of those things that happens, with nobody to blame.

Out of the smouldering pile of rubble came a determined voice: 'We will rebuild'. The voice was that of Bishop Colm O'Reilly. But it was a formidable challenge. The Celtic Tiger, during which we all thought we were God, had skulked away and we were left licking our financial wounds. Not a great time for restoration. But the human spirit once committed is indomitable. And so restoration began. Luckily, some far-seeing individual saw the need to film the restoration work as it progressed, and what a brilliant idea that was. The restoration took five years and in 2014 the people of Longford reopened their beautiful cathedral. As I sat enthralled watching the TV documentary of the amazing restoration, I decided that one day I would go to Longford to see St Mel's for myself. A rebuilt dream is an inspirational sight. It had taken me four years to get there, but finally here I was outside Longford cathedral.

When you step into the front porch of St Mel's you are almost overpowered by the amazing photographs of the burnt-out shell. You are surrounded by them. It is a wonderful photographic record of an awful event, a stark reminder of the devastation that faced the restoration effort. These graphic photographs tower around you, stretching from floor to ceiling, and you can almost smell the smoke.

On pushing open the entrance door into the main

building, my first impression was of a slightly scaled-down model to the version that I had in my head. As often happens, the TV cameras had exaggerated the scale. So I readjusted my inner perception. But then the towering pillars up along the aisles suddenly extended my walled-in thinking. Those pillars are mighty structures and raise your vision upwards.

Lest I be perplexed by the enormity of all that was to be absorbed, I decided to rein in my focus, furnish myself with a guide book, and concentrate on the immediate. Directly inside the main entrance door, the baptismal font rises elegantly out of an octagonal ceramic base of many shades of blue, giving the impression of water flowing around the font. To the right of it – and here I learnt a new word – is the evangelarium, which holds the Book of the Gospels. This one is a crystal glass showcase standing on a white marble column. It displayed the text of the Sunday Gospel of that week. To the left is a similar stand – and here I learnt another new word – the aumbry, holding three crystal vessels of rich colours containing the holy oils. These three elegantly sculpted statements make an impressive introduction to the cathedral.

Slightly overawed by the grandeur around me, I stood back to absorb the building in its entirety. It was a lot to take in. My eyes were again drawn to the magnificent pillars that pick up the colours of the ceramic pool of water around the baptismal font and seem to carry these colours upwards to the stained-glass windows high above my vision and on to the barrel-vaulted ceiling. The windows were – and here I learnt yet another new word – clerestory windows, which means that they are above eye level and near the ceiling. My initial reaction was what a pity to have them up so high and almost out of sight, though in another way I could see that they were indicative of the higher and out-of-sight inner mysteries of a sacred building. Though not totally visible from the floor, they cast light upwards onto the roof, and even from far down below, at ground level, their rich imagery lights up the decorative heritage plasterwork of the ceiling.

The windows down at eye level, however, are totally visible and breathtaking in their bright brilliance. There are four of them along each side of the cathedral, and they set the whole place aglow. Far removed from the elaborate traditional church windows, these windows suggest giant gossamer wings of floating birds in the most gorgeous, delicate, uplifting colours. Giving the sense of the outside coming inside, they light up the entire building with a heavenly glow. The sanctuary is a sea of marble waves and the magnificent organ is recessed into the high walls above it. To the right is a Pieta side-chapel and here, on a rostrum at the entrance, was a pad with a rota of names on it.

In this side-chapel some people were praying and as I walked around the cathedral I noticed that people came and went. It was obvious that this was an organised Perpetual Adoration, and I wondered if it was a weekly or daily occurrence. I would have liked to have talked to one of the people about their cathedral, but was reluctant to intrude.

However, just as I was abandoning the desire to talk with a local person, a priest walked quietly up a side aisle and went into what was obviously the sacristy behind the altar. He came back out almost immediately and as he came down the side aisle I placed myself in his path. I told him that I was a visitor and just wanted to talk about the cathedral. His face lit up with a welcoming smile and it was obvious that he was delighted to do so. In the course of our exchange I enquired if he was attached to the parish, and he smiled and told me, 'I was bishop here when we had the fire.' Then I recognised the kindly face of the man who had declared, 'We will rebuild'. As I had watched the restoration of the building on TV, I had judged him to be the soothing oil that had seen this tremendous undertaking through without conflict. Restoring any church is challenging, but restoring a historic cathedral, with many architects, artists, sculptors, stone masons and builders involved, must have been an undertaking requiring the wisdom of Solomon and the patience of Job. Undoubtedly, there had been some big egos on board, but looking into the wise and kindly face of Bishop Colm O'Reilly, one could understand how this calm and patient man would have poured oil on any artistic troubled waters. I was so glad to have met him as he added a human touch to my visit, because, while great churches are important, when all is said and done it is we, the people of God, who are the Church.

The Pope

Whether we heard that the World Meeting of Families was to take place during August 2018 we in Innishannon decided that though many of us would not be in the RDS, Croke Park or Knock, we could still be part of the gathering. So it was decided that on the first night of this six-day event, which was Tuesday, 21 August, we would have an all-night silent vigil in our own church in solidarity with the main event in Dublin.

Like all parishes, our parish is made up of many different families and all together we are a strong community family; this is evident when we gather on the occasions of funerals, fund-raisers and all kinds of parish gatherings. So we decided to gather as a parish family to be part of the World Meeting of Families. Not everybody could be in Dublin to share in this world event, but our community could still be part of it in spirit. In any case, many of us felt that the Church in today's Ireland is more about the parish community than the global.

This parish, like all rural parishes, is made up of a number of townlands, and in our parish small groups of these townlands cluster to form what we call 'station areas'. In each of these station areas, Mass is celebrated annually in one of the houses and all the neighbours gather, a longstanding tradition in rural Ireland. We call it 'The Stations'. It is a sociable community gathering, which, as well as being a religious occasion, is an opportunity for newcomers, if they wish, to get to know their neighbours.

The plan for our night vigil was that it would begin with Mass at 9pm and finish with another Mass at 7am, and during the intervening hours the people from the different station areas would gather for an allotted time and stay silently for an hour, or for as long as they desired.

Lists of the townlands with their designated hour were distributed at the Sunday Masses and placed on the church doors and announced at all the Masses. The lists of the names of the different townlands tell the story of these places, the old historic names almost like a narrative poem: Leighmoney, Shanagore, Rathnaroughy, Farnagow, Knockroe, Coolculitha, each name containing the history of its ancient roots. What a loss to the richness of our culture it would be if these ancient, meaningful names ever went out of use and were forgotten. One of the pluses of that now long-forgotten and odious Church custom of calling off the altar at Sunday Mass the names of the people of the different townlands and the amount that they contributed to the parish funds was that these beautiful old names became familiar to the ears of the children and indeed to all of the congregation. Many a new curate stumbled over the complexities of their pronuncation, much to the amusement of their congregation off whose tongues these names rolled like water over mossy stones. And in time, he too mastered the musical flow of the names.

On the Tuesday night as I walked up the hill to our church, I wondered how many people would come and was glad to see a large number of cars in the carpark. Inside the door was a table laden with the special candles issued to celebrate the World Meeting of Families and we were invited to take one home with us. It was a joyful Mass, with the congregation joining the choir in uplifting hymns, and our priest, Fr Finbarr, giving an encouraging talk on the many complexities and challenges facing families in today's Ireland.

When Mass was over and the bulk of the congregation had filed out, the church quietened down. The lights were lowered, and lighted candles placed on the altar, with a row of the special World Meeting of Families candles in front. There is something about candlelight that calms people, and slowly a sense of peace and tranquility descended on the church. Many people remained on in silent prayer. Soon they were joined by parishioners from the allocated townlands. Silence prevailed. The only sound to be heard was the occasional opening and closing of the back door as people came and went. Later, as I walked down the hill, the moon was high in the sky and I thought what a lovely night for a silent vigil. The hour allocated to our village was 2am to 3am, so before going to bed I set my alarm for 1.45am.

When I came back up at 2am there were many cars in the carpark and on entering the church I was welcomed by a sense of togetherness, tranquility and peace. In the semi-darkness people were silhouetted against the candlelit altar. A gathering of neighbours in silent prayer is something very special. The hour slipped by quickly and I was loath to leave the restful atmosphere, so I stayed on until the hard seat began to tell me that it was time to go. I went back down the hill and before going to bed set the alarm for 6.45am, and the next time that I walked up the hill a new day had dawned. Many people who had come during the night came back again for the 7am morning Mass.

In the church after the night of silent prayer there was a deep sense of restfulness. Buildings seem to absorb the essence of what goes on within their walls and an activity leaves behind an atmosphere of peace or turmoil, as the case may be. The walls of many old buildings become memory stones and forever retain the imprint of what went on there. On visiting the concentration camp at Dachau some years ago, I was chilled to the marrow of my bones as I walked there. The stones seemed to have absorbed the horrors of the past and this still permeated the atmosphere. In old churches, I find, there is a sense of peace and we usually feel an inclination to whisper rather than disturb the silence with the discord of sudden sound. Silence is rare and precious in today's world. As I came down the hill after Mass I felt energised by an inner peace. Meditation calms the inner being and rekindles our sense of harmony with the world and our fellow humans.

For the World Meeting of Families, the Pope was flying into Dublin on Saturday morning and leaving on Sunday night. His short visit was causing much controversy. Since the previous visit of Pope John Paul II in 1979 our Church had been rocked from within by the scandal of child sex abuse. This had led to disillusionment for many and a huge anger amongst people that the abuse, instead of being stamped out, had been covered up to save the institution. In the week of the Pope's arrival, fresh revelations of child sex abuse and cover-up erupted within the Church in America. The laity were dismayed, and uncertain as to how it was all going to unfold. Some saw the Pope as not effectively doing his job. There was also annoyance about the role of women in the Church and the Church's attitude to the LGBT community. For others, the Pope was Christ's vicar on earth and a sacred figure within the Church. All this led to conflicting attitudes about his visit to Ireland. It was an intriguing and challenging time for everyone and one could not but wonder how the visit was going to go, and what would be the general reaction.

Because I was fascinated by the whole saga I decided that in the days leading up to the Pope's visit I would keep myself well informed by reading up on everything, and watching and listening to all TV and radio programmes relevant to the visit. Two programmes were very interesting. One was hosted by former president Mary McAleese, and she went around Ireland and interviewed different families with a view to ascertaining the relevance of the Church in their lives. Another, hosted by Mick Peelo, did likewise and he also handed out Papal encyclicals, asking people to read them and consider if they could live up to the Pope's expectations. He came back later to discuss their opinions. In these two programmes we got the reactions of ordinary people, which was fascinating; the media are not always representative of the feelings of the people.

On the Saturday and Sunday of the visit, I decided to park myself in front of the TV and watch all the proceedings. I remember Gay Byrne once saying that unless you see or hear it for yourself, do not believe it! So I decided to see it and hear it for myself. It was a lovely, bright, sunny morning when the Pope's plane touched down in Dublin airport, where there was a clutter of dignitaries of Church and state to receive him. The little daughter of the Minister for Foreign Affairs, Simon Coveney, presented the Pope with a posy of flowers – later we learnt that at the last minute she got stage fright and had to be encouraged to do the needful with the promise of a kitten! The kitten was later called Francis. Lucky kitten!

Then on to Áras an Uachtaráin where the Pope was greeted by the President amidst a flurry of hand-shaking, and he planted a tree just behind the back door – not buried in the depths of the garden like Queen Victoria's tree – and then to the Mansion House, where the audience represented the political, cultural and social life of Ireland. There the Taoiseach welcomed the Pope in a thoughtful and well-executed speech, and the Pope responded with an apology for the past failings of the Church.

Next he went to the Pro-Cathedral, and he sat in silent prayer in front of the altar where a lighted candle stands in memory of the all those who suffered child abuse at the hands of the Church. The cathedral was filled with young married couples who then welcomed the Pope, their faces filled with love and joy. It was obvious that these couples were devout Catholics who were delighted to welcome the Pope into their midst. Then he travelled in the pope-mobile through the streets of Dublin, where he received a rapturous welcome, to the Capuchin Day Care Centre where every day hundreds of people are provided with meals. Here he blossomed into the shepherd amongst his flock. Later he had a private meeting with the victims of child sex abuse, which was probably a harrowing experience for all concerned.

That evening in Croke Park there was no competition for an all-Ireland medal as everyone there was on the winning team. The park was alive with the enthusiasm of a hand-clapping faithful, who were entertained by a joyous show of rock-concert standards. The set was impressive and the ever-changing backdrops riveting in their vibrancy and epic proportions. The audience received the musicians, choirs and performers with huge enthusiasm and delight, but when the Pope appeared in the pope-mobile all attention swung to him – it was obvious that he was the main act of the night. Having again apologised for the past failings of the Church, he sat back and obviously enjoyed the events that were focused on giving him a flavour of Irish life.

The following morning I turned on the television to a rain-drenched Knock where the West was awake and alive with colourful umbrellas and happy-faced people, whose enthusiasm was not in the least bit dampened by the pouring rain. But then, I suppose, if you grew up in the misty mountains of the West of Ireland you soon got accustomed to such weather conditions. On this wet Sunday morning in August, though the rain was pouring down, the sun was shining in the hearts of the people at Knock. The Pope visited the Chapel of the Apparition at Knock and prayed quietly, again apologising for the failings of the Church. He then said the Angelus. It was a whirlwind visit for which Knock had been preparing for months, and on the day they glowed in readiness. Their parish priest, Fr Richard Gibbons, was totally at ease with his people and his guest, whom he obviously loved and respected. He was right man in the right place.

After Knock it was the grand finale that afternoon in the Phoenix Park where the Pope celebrated Mass. Due to the rain, the Phoenix Park was a sea of colourful umbrellas from beneath which happy faces smiled with delight. When the pope-mobile arrived, the sea of umbrellas swept in its direction and I held my breath in case their enthusiasm would swirl people in front of the vehicle. But the vigilant security guards saw to it that the Pope made it without incident to the altar. There he celebrated Mass, during which he again apologised for the sins of the Church.

A sea of white umbrellas escorted the Ministers of the Eucharist distributing Holy Communion to the huge congregation. It was a daunting undertaking, but all was achieved in due course. After Mass the Pope met with the Irish bishops, and then left for the airport to fly back to Rome.

When the Aer Lingus plane disappeared into the clouds I rose from my couch and went for a long walk. I wondered what affect his visit had on the members of his flock who are still trying to cope in the aftermath of the tsunami of sex abuse which washed around them. And what did his visit mean to the shrinking number of stalwart priests who are now trying to pick up the pieces and keep the Church functioning for the faithful all around them? I got the answer to that question when our local priest, Fr Finbarr, later wrote an article for *Candlelight*, our village journal. Here is an extract:

> His presence gave us hope. For me, present that night, that was the overriding feeling or emotion that I felt. He gave us hope.
>
> 'Please', 'Thank you', 'I'm sorry', were the words that Pope Francis said he would like to write on the

door of every home. That night in Croke Park, many of us present felt empowered by Pope Francis to make our world a more just and better place to live in. The concert was brilliant, the testimonies of the families from around the world that spoke to us of their struggles, challenged us and made us realise how blessed we are. But for me, Pope Francis' presence filled me with hope, that we are all cherished by God in a very unique way.

I travelled home to Innishannon that night filled with emotion that I was blessed to be present in Croke Park on the Saturday evening.

The Ring-around

On a morning in early October every year, Maureen, Mary and I sit around the kitchen table to lay out *Candlelight*. This year we were doing it for the thirty-fifth time. Over those years we have had some hilarious moments and also times when we wondered if we might find ourselves running up the steps of the High Court. But so far so good! Even though the writers pen the words, we could be held responsible for the end product. But we see *Candlelight* as the voice of the people and so we do very little editing, although Maureen occasionally warns us: 'There's a rat in high heels waiting out there!' What an image – but so far he has not come out of his rat hole.

I'm not sure how the term 'laying out' evolved for preparing a publication, but would imagine that its origin has some connection with our final laying out of a body at the end of this earthly sojourn. As we begin our *Candlelight* layout, we have no idea of the overall picture, but it emerges as we do word-checks and try to get a general flavour of the contents. We

aim for a good mix of past, present, serious, humorous and seasonal. But that all depends on what comes in! A bit like making a cake, it's all about the ingredients.

Weeks before comes the ring-around, or as Maureen terms it: 'Rounding up the usual suspects.' But whatever we may call it, the ring-around is an absolutely vital exercise when attempting to get anything done in the parish, from planting trees to doing a big clean-up. Even in this high-tech world of modern technology, nothing beats the eye-to-eye contact or the human voice on the phone. Contact by other means may be dismissed as applying to 'them' or 'ye', so the direct human touch is far more effective.

The ring-around for *Candlelight* begins in late August or early September. It can be highly entertaining and never ceases to bring a smile to my face. It can often lead, too, to long drawn-out, fascinating conversations. Most people protest in horror at the fact that this time of year has actually come around again, and I have to assure them that I had nothing to do with the speed of time! Then, we get on with the matter on hand. You sometimes get the feeling that they would be delighted were you to write the article for them. Charlie Madden was always an exception to this rule and his reaction on hearing me was yet again heart-warming: 'Well, Alice, how are you? I was expecting you and do you know what I have decided on this year for *Candlelight* …' and so a long conversation would evolve that carried us around the whole parish past and present until finally we came back to Charlie's article and he waxed eloquent on his chosen subject. He had grown up in this parish and for years was part of its bone structure, and now ran a pub in a neighbouring parish. He knew the world and its wife, was a witty conversationalist and could pour out his words on paper with free abandon. Such people are gold dust for magazines like *Candlelight*, or indeed, for any publications.

But often a reluctant starter can produce a gem. Paudie Palmer is one of our GAA pundits who pours out match commentaries, interlaced with background family lore, over the airways; he is our own Micheál Ó Muircheartaigh. His reaction on being asked to write an article is always mock horror; he reacts as if he is being forced to face a firing squad or to do Lough Derg. But I know that he can produce the goods and he knows that I know. And this year again he eventually capitulated with great good humour, and a super article duly arrived. Another contributor reacts as if stepping into the labour ward, but she too duly delivers. But one reaction that is very common is the reluctance of people to put pen to paper in case what they write might be criticised by others. When I asked one man why this was important to him, he told me, 'You wouldn't understand, because you don't care what people think of you.' That softened my cough for me!

But one way to avoid this dilemma is to write under a pen name, which one of our writers has done for years, and this year she came up with an article that might give you a flavour of the variety that can sometimes come in for *Candlelight*. Here's this year's article:

Gone Before Morning

When I answered the knock on the front door of my Bed and Breakfast, two tanned cyclists were on the doorstep. It was a bit early in the season for cyclists, but these two were obviously seasoned travellers, well equipped with guides and maps and the usual trappings of experienced bikers. I checked them into a twin-bedded room, and when they had settled in and divested themselves of their travelling gear, they joined me in the sitting room for tea and scones. They introduced themselves as Andrew and Bert, and had over the previous twenty years come across from England and cycled the highways and byways of Ireland, and enjoyed every minute of it. Andrew was tall, thin and fit as a fiddle, while Bert, the elder of the two, was shorter and of a stockier build. Their wives were not into cycling, so Bert's wife had gone on a sun holiday while Andrew's wife was taking part in a ballroom-dancing competition.

When I later returned to the kitchen and relayed all this information to my husband, Jack, he rolled his eyes to heaven and declared that they needed to have their heads examined and that their wives sounded far more sensible. My Jack takes the car the short journey down town every morning to collect the paper, so that tells a lot about his attitude to fitness.

The following morning I prepared a good breakfast for my two pleasant guests. My Jack, who is not a morning person, was still fast asleep in bed. The rashers were just beginning to sizzle nicely under the grill when a hesitant knock came on the kitchen door. Then Bert put his head around the door. His face told me that something was not right. 'Sorry to bother you so early, but I think that my friend is dead.' I remember thinking, Who but an Englishman could be so restrained in the circumstances? But as I am neither English nor a man, I reacted in a typical Irish female fashion: 'O Jesus, Mary and Holy Saint Joseph, he can't be!' I screamed, and turned off the grill (later I gave myself great credit for having that presence of mind). 'I'm afraid so,' Bert said apologetically. I ran to the bedroom hoping against hope for an incorrect diagnosis of Andrew's condition. But no such luck. There was Andrew, looking relaxed and restful, and quite pleased

to have gone wherever he now was. I gave him a gentle
shake to make sure that he was not in a yoga trance or
deep in meditation. But no doubt about it, Andrew was
definitely dead.

So what do I do now? I asked myself. Where do I
go? Whom do I send for? All these questions jumped
into my mind as I quickly realised that this was *my*
emergency and that I had to get a grip on myself and
handle it to the best of my ability. Then I suddenly
remembered that Jack was still asleep in bed. I went
through that bedroom door like a bullet and gave him
the first hard belt that he had ever got from me in
our years of not-always-harmonious bliss. He shot up
in bed, demanding in amazement, 'What the blazes is
wrong with you?'

'Andrew in No 3 is dead,' I shouted at him.

He was out of bed like a scalded cat. I ran back
down the corridor to make sure that Bert was all right
and persuaded him to come into the sitting room
where I reversed him into a comfortable armchair and
went to make him a cup of tea. In the kitchen Jack
was wondering who to call first: the doctor, the guards,
the priest or the undertaker? With the best of female
logic, I advised him to call the doctor as the rest were
not on our calling list. The doctor came and pronounced Andrew definitely dead and complained that
this would require a lot of form filling for him, which

I told him sharply to get on with as the last thing I needed was a dead body in residence. He instructed that the next step was to call the Guards, which I did. The Boys in Blue promptly arrived, three of them. They were wonderful. First they went to check on Andrew and then chatted with Bert as he sipped his cup of tea unaware that he was being interrogated Irish style, then they asked Bert to stay with me until after the coroner had come and done the needful. When I heard the word 'coroner' my head went into a spin. I visualised my best bedroom being transformed into an operating theatre to ascertain the reason why Andrew had taken an impulsive urge to leave us all behind. But the Sargeant, on seeing my look of horror, told me calmly, 'I will ring the Cottage Hospital to send the ambulance to take the body up there and the coroner will do the needful in their morgue.' The ambulance came quickly and shifted Andrew up the road to the hospital. So far so good.

But that was only the beginning! Then the tally started. Bert got on the phone to Mrs Andrew to be told that as she was now in the final of the waltz- ing competition travel at this time would be highly inconvenient, and would Bert take care of everything and do whatever it was that needed to be done? To say that I was a bit taken aback by her reaction was put- ting it mildly, but to give me credit I kept my mind to myself and gave Jack a threatening look to put a stitch on his lip, and he got my message loud and clear. Mrs Andrew's message, however, had an amazing affect on Bert. He sprang into new life at her decision to leave all the arrangements in his hands and declared that Andrew had always wanted a DIY funeral and this was the perfect opportunity to put his wish into action.

This was all news to Jack and myself. We had never heard of a DIY funeral in Ireland, but Bert assured us that it was becoming a big thing in England and he was all in favour of it. Just like making your own beer or your own kitchen cupboards, he told us, you cut out the middle man, no need for him as he makes all the money out of the customer's needs. Bert was full of enthusiasm for his new project. While we waited for the results from the coroner, Bert began his pursuit of the DIY funeral. Our local undertaker was not enthused with his idea and refused to sell him a coffin without the follow-up services. Bert was not put off by this, and soon found the address of the nearest coffin supplier, and Jack offered to drive Bert to this man who could solve the problem.

With their departure I sat down to review the situation, but all the comings and goings had alerted the neighbours and Sean, our local flower, fruit and veg man, arrived to investigate. When Bert and Jack came back with the makings of a coffin sticking out of the boot Sean joined them in assembling it out in the back yard. Apparently a DIY model was cheaper than the finished product, and Bert had gone for economy.

That night we carried Andrew's coffin in one of Mick's large fruit vans up to the hospital morgue. There, Andrew, who'd had a heart attack, had been beautifully laid out by the nurses, who, thinking he needed a touch of the sacred, had entwined a rosary beads in his fingers. Bert promptly removed it, smilingly saying, 'No need for worry beads because Andrew was not a worrier.'

Next on the agenda was getting Andrew back to his dancing wife. But now that Bert was into his stride there was no end to his resourcefulness and Sean was in the export business, so between them they soon had all the required arrangements made to fly Andrew back home from the nearest airport. The following morn-ing we loaded up Andrew's coffin into one of Sean's fruit vans, keeping it firmly in position with plants, trees and bags of spuds. As we travelled to the airport behind Sean's van, beautifully painted along both sides with gorgeous flowers, I thought how much nicer than a drab hearse this was. Maybe there was a lot to be said for a DIY funeral.

When I read this article I rang the scribe, who did keep guests, and enquired, 'Did that really happen?'

'You couldn't make that up, could you?' she asked.

Honourable People

Before having my breakfast I popped into the shop next door to get the morning paper – yes, some of us fossils still read newspapers! To my surprise, Martina at the check-out handed me a bag, saying, 'A woman left that in for you and said something about her daughter and flowers, but I did not quite get the full story.' 'I wonder what that's all about?' I said, taking the lovely, colourful bag, and heading back into my kitchen. I placed the bag on the table and viewed it with curiosity. The vibrant bag of red, yellow and green was in itself a happy statement. Full of curiosity, I eased open the top of the bag and inside was a beautiful box of chocolates and a box of luxury biscuits.

Wow! What is this for? I wondered, hoping that there was an explanatory note. If not, I would be forever guessing. But in with the boxes was an envelope with my name on it. I opened the envelope and inside was a short note, headed 'Tidy Towns'. It said: 'I'd like to take this time to apologise for the event that occurred on the night of the 25th August which led to your flower tubs being damaged. Thank you so much for being so understanding. Thanks again …' It was signed, but with no address.

I re-read it and re-read it and tried hard to remember the 25th of August. What on earth had happened on the 25th of August? My brain was a blank. What could possibly have happened on that night to lead to this generosity to Tidy Towns? I tried hard to recall that date, but nothing immediately came to mind. It was over two months back, and I rattled my memory to try to resurrect a happening involving flowers and damage. Whatever had happened, it was after Gardens and Galleries, because prior to that we were all on red alert about village maintenance and if anything damaging flowers and pots had happened there would have been such a big hoo-ha it would not have been so easily forgotten. But once Gardens and Galleries was done and dusted we all relaxed a little. A bit like a team after winning the All Ireland.

Ours is a very busy village. Being a main artery into West Cork, we have a constant flow of through traffic and over the years we have had the odd mishap, but thankfully nothing of lasting or dire consequence. Unsociable behaviour is not a problem either, and this is due in no small measure to the fact that we have a resident Garda, Tadhg, and his wife, Niamh, both involved in parish affairs, who, with their young family, live in the barracks at the eastern end of the village. For this we are extremely grateful and even though Tadhg is attached to nearby Bandon station, it is a great plus for the village to have him living here in the midst of us and involved in everything that goes on.

As I rattled my brain to try to recall the events of the past summer that might have caused upset to Tidy Towns, I recalled one night when a busload of teenagers had disembarked at the corner and called into the local pub. This happens occasionally. Later, a slightly inebriated teenager emerged from the pub tottering on a pair of dangerously high heels and swayed around a flower trough at the corner. She uprooted an elegant Cordyline and proceeded to waltz with it around the trough. At times it looked as if she might topple over, but just as it appeared inevitable that she would upend into the trough she regained her balance and became perpendicular just in time. When the dance was over, she dumped her partner on the street corner from where I retrieved it following day and tucked it back into its snug bed. Was it possible that this teenager, on sober recollection, remembered what had happened and wanted to make amends? Highly unlikely! This, I decided, seemed more the act of a contrite mother, but then how would a contrite mammy know of the midnight waltz? So that was out.

Then, all of a sudden, it came to me like a bolt from the blue. Suddenly the whole forgotten picture clicked into my mind like the pieces of a jigsaw. It should have come to me straight away because at the time it was a bit of a calamity. It was, of course, the scatter of the tubs at the barrack corner which had happened early one morning in August.

That morning I got a phone call from John, who lives at that end of the village. 'The place down here is like a war zone,' he announced. As he is prone to exaggeration, I downgraded that to 'a bit of a mess'. 'What happened?' I asked him. 'Someone must have taken the corner too fast and shot in over the edge in front of the market house and scattered tubs and earth all over the place,' he told me. 'Are the tubs broken?' I asked. 'They're in pure shit,' he proclaimed. 'Come down and see for yourself.'

Unfortunately his assessment was pretty accurate. There was a scatter of earth, tubs and plants all along the street in front of the Old Market House. On look-ing at it one realised that the car involved could not have come through this melee unscratched. Then I saw that the car was actually parked further up the street and did look a bit battle-scarred after its encounter with the tubs. I rang Tadhg, to be told that the matter had been reported by the car owner to the barracks in Bandon, with an offer to make good any expense incurred for Tidy Towns and a promise to return and clean up. That immediately made me feel better. It restores your faith in human nature when people act with responsibility and decency. And there would, in fact, be very little expense for Tidy Towns as the tubs had been well past their sell-by date and most of the plants would recover. They had left a phone number, which I rang.

A lovely man answered and told me that his daughter had come through our village late the previous night and that on rounding the barrack corner she had been dazzled by the lights of an oncoming truck and had swerved to avoid it, hence the resulting accident. He offered to come and clean up and pay for any damages incurred. It was a wet, miserable day and not a day for brushing the streets, so I told him to let it be and that our Tidy Towns members and the FÁS lads would tidy up, and assured him that there were no expenses involved. I felt that they had had enough trauma with the accident, without us adding to the situation. The following day we cleaned up the mess and replaced the tubs with barrels that we got free from a local farmer. Then we forgot all about it!

But not so the family involved. At the following Tidy Towns meeting I produced their boxes of biscuits and chocolates, and read the letter. People like that girl and her father make the world a better place.

A few years ago we had another such incident in the village when an early-morning commuter failed to observe a red light and had to swerve to avoid hitting an oncoming car, and in the process shot out of control onto the pavement outside my front door, resulting in somersaulting a stone trough, which cracked in two, scattering shrubs and earth along the street. A total mess to behold! However, a local farmer came good with a replacement redundant cattle trough, and that night as we replanted the new trough the apologetic culprit, who had already reported the accident to the barracks, appeared and offered to make amends. We assured him that there was no need, mainly because he had been honourable enough to report the accident. Later, in gratitude, he made beautiful fairy doors for our wood.

Which all goes to show that Shylock did not get it right and that random acts of kindness do bear fruit.

Living the Dream

Hold fast to dreams
For if dreams die
Life is a broken-winged bird
That cannot fly.

We were on the road to Ballyfin, my daughter and I. The realisation of my long-held dream was about to unfold. Then, unexpectedly, tiny seeds of apprehension began to sprout doubts in my mind. Would it fulfil my high expectations? Could this place possibly live up to years of harbouring a secret dream to see it? Now that the dream was finally about to be unveiled I was having last-minute nerves. Had I created a beautiful bubble that was about to burst? Would the reality be far less than the mirage that I had enshrined in my mind?

Then we arrived at the gate. Two years previously I had made a detour to pass by this very gate to have my photograph taken in front of it, thinking then

that I would never get to see all that was inside. I had decided that a photograph of the gate was as near as I would ever get to Ballyfin, but at least I would have that photograph. But then my big birthday came along and my crew decided to put an end to their mother's constant chanting about beautiful Ballyfin.

Now, as Lena spoke to the hidden voice in the pillar, I waited in anticipation for the black gates to unlock. As they slowly swung open I suddenly got a feeling that the gates of heaven were opening wide to allow me in. All that was missing was St Peter. But could he at any moment step out of the gate lodge, either to beckon me forward into a heavenly vision or banish me to a lesser place of disillusionment!

But no Peter appeared, only large trees that lined the curving driveway that seemed to go on forever and ever as we made our way slowly towards whatever lay hidden ahead. The massive, ancient trees along the way were interspersed with plantations of young trees ready to take the green baton of Ballyfin into the future. Here you could see that the past and the future were being beautifully blended.

Then at last we came around the unveiling corner, and there, before us, in all its magnificence, stood Ballyfin. It was an imposing mansion, imperious, impressive, surrounded by sweeping lawns and fronted by an enormous lake reflecting the luxuriant woodlands and mountains. All the surroundings were laid out in homage to the great house – the lake, the lawns and the woods were created specially to enhance her dominance. The Slieve Bloom Mountains alone had been here before her, but even they were genuflecting into her lake as she held royal court in the midst of all this natural beauty.

When we got out of the car at the foot of the wide flight of steps leading up to her throne, I felt like bowing in homage to this impressive lady, but before I could genuflect, my hand was firmly grasped by a pleasant, friendly-faced young woman who warmly welcomed us to Ballyfin. She smilingly escorted us up the steps into the grand front hall where a huge log fire glowed and two elegant glasses of sparkling champagne floated in front of us.

We had stepped back into another world. This was the world into which English landlords had poured their tenants' money to create great houses such as this. Some of those fine houses were burnt in the struggle for independence, but luckily others had escaped. But the maintenance of many that had survived was beyond the financial capacity at the time and they also finished up in ruins. Others were acquired by wealthy families who restored and maintained them as private residences.

Ballyfin, however, wound its way down a different

avenue. It was lucky to have escaped burning, as the astute owner of the time had placed a caretaker with republican sympathies in charge, and he had manipulated the survival of Ballyfin. That luck continued when it was acquired by the Patrician Brothers for use as a school. Even though the Brothers could not afford to provide the maintenance required, they had an appreciation for the integrity of the building, and all the original fireplaces and some of the grand features remained untouched. However, eventually leaking roofs and rotting floors forced them to say goodbye to this enormous old house that had become a millstone around their necks. And again, Ballyfin was lucky when, with the departure of the Patrician Brothers, along came visionaries who saw other possibilities in the preservation and restoration of the building. It was an overwhelming and daunting task that took nine years of constant dedication to complete. Luckily for Ballyfin, finance was not a problem as the possibility is that the owners may never get their money back. But their motivation was probably never about the money. It was a dream and a challenge. They had the vision and as a result of that vision Ballyfin was saved and destined to survive and blossom again in a new era. The landlord era was over, but this fine house and magnificent trees remained to be preserved for posterity.

And what a treasure it was to preserve and make available to anyone lucky enough to come here to enjoy and savour. And 'savour' is the operative word. Ballyfin is full of treasures from the past, blended skillfully with elegant ease into the comforts of the present. It is a meandering delight to the senses to wander around the gracious rooms where you sink into supremely comfortable old-world couches, full of warmth and cosiness. The whole ambience of the house exudes welcome, relaxation and ease. Here the peace of silence is broken only by the occasional crackling of the many log fires.

During an informative tour of the house we were led from one visual delight to another. Lionel, who had worked on the restoration of Ballyfin, was an enlightened and entertaining host. He had no need to study the history of this house as he had absorbed and become part of it during the restoration. It was obvious that he knew and loved every stone of this old building. That is one of the secrets of Ballyfin: it is cared for and loved by staff who delight in sharing its pleasures with their guests. They are proud of their house and enjoy showing its treasures. It was an inspirational decision by the owners to invite past pupils of the school and craftspeople who had worked on the restoration to stay on if they wished and become part of the Ballyfin team. In this way a well informed and inspired team was created to introduce the guests to a unique and enriching experience. You feel that you have slipped into a gracious welcoming home rather than a hotel. The ghosts of past history have been laid peacefully to rest and Ballyfin has been rebirthed into a new era.

Off the grand entrance hall is the Whispering Room. I had never heard of a whispering room and it intrigued me. It has to be an architectural wonder. It is constructed so that when you stand in one corner of the room and whisper, somebody standing in the far distant corner can clearly hear you due to the curved design of the ceiling. This room was designed to be of assistance to the landlord's agent when doing a deal. If the negotiations were floundering and he wanted to move things on, he suggested to his clients that they retreat into a far corner to confer between themselves. To give them the added sense of security of not being overheard by him, he then moved away from them into the opposite corner. However, what they did not know was that in his corner he could hear the whole exchange as clearly as if they were standing beside him. An utterly fascinating feature that has to be experienced to be believed. Also, when you stand under the enormous, elegant chandelier in the centre of this room, your voice echoes above you.

Beyond the Whispering Room is an elegant staircase, with shining brass bannisters, that curves up along a high wall from where portraits of the departed Coote family gaze down. The Cootes were the last family of the landlord era to live here. This hallway opens into the saloon where magnificent portraits of two elegant ladies in flowing gold gowns on either side of the great mantelpiece give the aura of another era. In this room the restored floor was made possible due to the fact that the last member of the Patrician brothers to leave Ballyfin led the restorers to one of the attics where boxes of the wooden panels, rescued by a foresightful Brother, had been stored by Mrs Barry, who had been the housekeeper when the house was a boarding school. What a far-seeing woman! In Ballyfin it is all about the story.

Later that night, sitting beside the fire, Pat, another member of the staff, told us that in Ballyfin he believes that you come out of your head and into your heart. He is right and it actually happens while you are totally absorbed enjoying the peace and quiet of the house. The silence of Ballyfin slowly unwinds your mind.

Off the library a secret door hidden in a bookcase leads into a little panelled corridor, which, in turn, opens into the restored dome-roofed conservatory, which is flooded with light and furnished with comfortable wicker tables and chairs. Two elegant marble figures draw your eyes upwards to the amazing intricacies of the fine glass panelling overhead. Because I had watched the delicate restoration on TV it was now a delight to see it. If you dine in here you enjoy the wonderful sound and view of a foaming waterfall cascading down a wide flight of stone steps and gushing forth though the mouths of six lions into a fountain, in which a massive stone figure reclines. Golf buggies and maps are available and you can drive around at your leisure, so Lena and I had an entertaining hour exploring the hidden wonders of Ballyfin demesne.

Later we retired to the cream-and-blue elegance of the Lady Catherine Coote room, which was our bedroom, where an enormous four-poster bed stood draped in a cascade of cream and white drapery. In the accompanying bathroom the comforts of the present day are seamlessly blended with the opulence of the past. If you open a secret door opposite the entrance to Lady Coote's bedroom you discover a narrow stone stairway leading down to what, in earlier days, were the servants' quarters; the steps are worn into a curve from years of trays being borne up from the kitchens. Those stairs now lead down to the ballroom, the swimming pool, sauna and treatments rooms. Changed times indeed!

The following morning after a breakfast of the best porridge that I have ever tasted, laced with Ballyfin honey and cream, and crunchy brown bread thatched with homemade marmalade and an unbelievable variety of fresh fruits, we took a step up in the world from the golf buggy when Lionel arrived at the front steps in a low-slung black carriage drawn by two beautiful white horses, Ben and Kitt, and treated us to an informative and highly entertaining tour. Ballyfin is surrounded by over six hundred acres of land, incorporating seven gate lodges, which are now being restored. Many acres around the house were originally maintained as pleasure gardens and one of the trees still standing since those days is an Irish oak, now four hundred years old. All along the way are plantations of young trees that will in time replace these ancient giants when they succumb to old age or stormy weather.

I loved the gardens, and was especially fascinated by Lady Catherine Coote's aviary, which housed her peacocks and other exotic birds; it makes for intriguing viewing with its built-in escape hatches along the base, and above them rows of little windows to provide the feathered residents with ease of access – these birds probably had a better home than some of the tenants! But then, Lady Catherine's philosophy in life was 'cost what it may', meaning no cost was spared. On another hill behind the house, a round tower flying the Irish tricolour is a challenging climb, but at the top you are rewarded for your efforts with a view of thirteen counties. The tour finished with a drive around the lake, across which impressive Ballyfin can be viewed in all its magnificence. The far-distant Slieve Bloom Mountains, off which the waters pour into the huge manmade lake, and the encircling luxuriant woodlands lend enchantment to the view.

We were reluctant to leave it all behind. But I felt enriched and blessed to have been afforded the privilege of visiting this wonderful old house and demense, with its ancient and varied history. You had to feel a debt of gratitude to the present owners for their vision in restoring and maintaining this amazing place. In their pursuit of perfection, they too had adopted Lady Catherine's philosophy: 'cost what it may'. It is wonderful that we have people who dream big dreams and selflessly put wings beneath them.

Ballyfin had lived up to – and above and beyond – all my expectations. It had taken me a long time to get there, but maybe the waiting years had fostered a greater sense of appreciation and gratitude. And I was glad to be able to report back to the extended family that their big birthday gift had been much appreciated, and was a huge success.

Winter Colour

I was dithering! My front-of-house window boxes, which had glowed vibrant with gorgeous, bright red geraniums all summer, were now slowly turning to a surly dark red. Though the greenery was still looking good, the flowers were sulking and turning black with frustration in the damp and chilly weather. It's hard to blame them. Geraniums need sun, and unfortunately our winter days do not provide for their needs. They were now an uninspiring sight. What to do with them was the question. If I opted to leave them outside, there were three possibilities. One was that they could survive and, with regular dead-heading over winter, could look all right – though if I were to be honest with myself, I might have to settle for half-all right. Secondly, they could be annihilated in one night by a harsh frost. Thirdly, should the weather come wet and murky, they could slowly succumb to prevailing conditions and simply rot. A sorry sight. Not one to lift the winter spirits.

The lazy me told the get-up-and-go me to let them

be. Sure, they will be grand, I told myself! But I knew in my inner core that I was only codding myself and that they would not be grand. And in my honest gardener's heart, I knew that full well. For a few weeks the two selves had an inner argument: to let be or not? And like most arguments, it was settled by another party, an independent arbitrator.

On a grey November day, walking down the street, I saw a window box glowing with exquisite, vibrant primulas. They were simply gorgeous and brought an instant smile to my face. They lit up my day. This was the answer. The lovely flowers beckoned me forward and encouraged action. I needed to give myself a good kick in the rear end and get myself moving. In winter we really need bright colours to keep us afloat. We need them then more than during the warm days of summer. Cheery window boxes lift our spirits on grey dismal days. They are almost a necessity.

It's amazing how, once a decision is made, all else falls into place. So I cracked into action. My first requirement was primulas. Loads of them! So I rang Donal in nearby St Patrick's, Upton, where he is helped by the residents, and supplies us all with summer and winter bedding plants. St Patrick's is a residential home for vulnerable adults and they are well cared for there. Amongst other activities, they grow plants, which we in the parish, and especially Tidy Towns, are glad to buy. Now, the primulas were available and at a very reasonable price, so that was the first fence cleared. The next step was the availability of my 'man for all seasons', John, who comes to my rescue when any job requiring muscle and stamina is taking place. John is a cheery, witty individual, with a wonderful work ethic, whose merry approach to life turns chores into light-hearted undertakings. He was available, so now all that was needed was a fine day.

In case at this point you think that we are talking about two or three window boxes, I need to tell you that there are, in fact, a lot of window boxes. This house was originally called the Corner House, which is self-explanatory, and has windows facing both the main street and the side street, at ground and first-floor levels. There are also hanging baskets. Hence all the self-questioning about the undertaking. It is no small job! But now that reluctance was eradicated, getting the job done was the name of the game.

The forecast was not great, but in late November you have to take what you get, so early one dreary morning before coming downstairs I lifted in the upstairs window boxes and put them on a table in a spare bedroom. No going back now!

After breakfast John and I got cracking. The first job was to bring down the previous winter/spring window boxes from the top of the garden where they had been parked in the grove out of sight since the previous May when they were replaced by the summer boxes. During the summer months they had been forgotten, so I was curious now as to their condition many months later. Each summer the survival rate varies. But now, once the debris of leaves and weeds was removed they seemed to be in good enough order, and on probing into the very moist earth I discovered that the many bulbs buried within were already beginning to show signs of life. It was an encouraging sight. That is the beauty of bulbs – they are survivors and come back year after year. What a great investment they are.

Once the boxes were ready, the next step was to collect the primulas, so into John's van we got and up the road to Upton, a few minutes' drive away. There the greenhouse was full of gorgeous primulas – red, yellow, pink and multi-coloured. No need for colour coordination as primulas all dance together in a delight of exuberance. We loaded up and paid up, and then headed down the road, into the backyard and we got cracking into action. Primula planting began and also we added more bulbs already acquired from Brian Perrott of West Cork Bulbs Centre, which is also in the parish. (Yes, I know we are a bit of a pain here in Innishannon, as we have everything!)

John brought in the ground-floor window boxes of

retiring geraniums and we set them aside for choice of storage to be decided later, when we opted for a sheltered site under a Pittosporum in a corner of the backyard. Next summer we will discover if this was a wise decision and if they have made it through the dark days of winter. Gardening is all about dancing with nature.

On the removal of flower boxes window sills are a sorry sight, so they needed a big scrub-down. Then, beginning with the front, ground-floor windows, the flower-box return began. The vibrant primulas brought colour along the street. Then the hanging baskets went back – I have a love/hate relationship with them as I believe that no self-respecting flower was meant to grow flying in mid-air, nevertheless I succumb to the need for colour along blank walls, especially on grey winter days.

When all was accomplished, I stood back and soaked up the delights of the beautiful colours. They brought life and vibrancy to the street and when viewed from inside the house they smiled back in at me through the windows. They will brighten up winter days. And also hidden within the boxes was the golden promise of delights yet to come when the snowdrops, crocuses, daffodils and tulips would sprout up and dance into life, brighten up winter days and herald in the first days of spring.

A Voice from
the Past

In today's world the arrival of a handwritten letter
is an occasion for celebration. In our hurried
society very few of us take the time to sit down and
actually write a letter. So to get one is rare and wonderful. And when such a letter comes from somebody
whom you have not seen or heard from for years –
and whom you may even have decided you will never
see or hear from again – such a letter stops you in your
tracks. It rolls back the years.

When I was a distracted young mother, for some
reason not altogether clear to me then or even now,
I occasionally found myself on Lough Derg island
for a pilgrimage weekend. That may sound as if I was
air-lifted on to that cold, bleak, barren corner of self-
inflicted misery, but not so. I may have gone there hes-
itantly and reluctantly, but the final decision to go was
mine and mine alone. I never encouraged anyone to
accompany me because I was afraid of their reaction

Alic

Deer

not remember
long the berg
Long talked
we
said that
not reflect

to cold, hunger and sleep deprivation. I did not want to become the first murder victim on Lough Derg.

On one particular occasion I was sitting on a hard rock at the edge of the lake trying to stay awake after the all-night vigil when I was joined by a pleasant-faced, happy man, who, unlike the rest of us, looked as if he was enjoying all the pleasures of a sun holiday. I had already met him on the bus up to the island and found him extremely good company, so now I smiled in welcome and made space for him on my rock. Good company at Lough Derg is vital to surviving that long, boring day of praying and fasting after a sleep-deprived night, when the hunger becomes obsessive and you begin to doubt your sanity.

Our subject of discussion on the bus had been the condition of our Church at the time, which was before the introduction of lay ministers, or, indeed, any lay participation whatsoever. We may think that we have a male-dominated Church nowadays, but it was more so back then in the mid-seventies, a situation that annoyed the blazes out of me. This man, Fr Jackie Power, was an Augustinian priest stationed in Cork, and he was very open to discussion about the state of the Church, which was rare enough at that time. So we settled down to a long exchange of ideas, during which I blew off a lot of frustration, and he listened attentively. I told him that I found the Church over-institutionalised, with not enough humanity, and that the priests were out of touch, with their long, boring sermons. He listened quietly and we agreed on more points than we disagreed. Finally, he said to me: 'You are very angry with the Church. Did you ever think of writing about it?' This was long before I had entered the public domain with my writing.

When I came home I thought about what he had said and wrote the following poem:

Back to Simplicity

Oh dedicated clergyman dressed in black
What a mighty Church is at your back
We are taught that by your hand
We must be led to your promised land,
Jesus is locked in your institutions
Of ancient laws and resolutions,
Buried so deep and out of sight
Sometimes we cannot see the light,
Behind huge walls that cost so much
Where simple things are out of touch.
But could it be he is not within
These walls so thick, with love so thin?
Does he walk on distant hills
Where long ago he cured all ills?
Is he gone to out to open places

To simple people, all creeds all races?
Is Jesus gone from off the altar,
Catching fish down by the water?
Is he with the birds amongst the trees
Gathering honey with the bees?
Could it be in this simple way
That God meant man to kneel and pray?

I then gave the poem to our local curate, Fr Seamus,
to read, and was a bit surprised at his reaction. 'Did
you ever think,' he asked me, 'that we too are caught
in the system?' His comment gave me food for
thought. Were the priests locked in and unable to get
out, while we were outside unable to get in? Was the
system so rigid that it was totally inflexible? Had this
system, like many others of its kind throughout the
world, though set up with vision and idealism, turned
into a self-destructive monster? I cannot now remember whether I sent the poem to Fr Power, who at
the time wrote an inspirational weekly column in the
Cork newspaper, the *Evening Echo*. We lost touch, but
I never quite forgot him.

Then years later, when we were unveiling a sculpture in our village of Billy, the local blacksmith, Billy's
family invited a friend to unveil the sculpture. His
name was Fr Power. I wondered if this could possibly
be the same man, and on the day of the unveiling

was delighted to discover that indeed it was. He was grey-haired and older, but still glowing with the same enthusiasm and zest for life. 'Do you remember me?' he asked. 'I never forgot you,' I told him.

It was a busy day with little time for talking, and that evening he went back to Waterford where he was then based and again we lost touch. But a few years later a neighbour of mine went to a funeral in Waterford where he was the officiating priest and the congregation was a mix of denominations, and when Holy Communion time came around Fr Power announced, 'Everyone is welcome to share.' He had not changed. His God had no compartments. Then, for many years, there was silence, and as he was now fairly old I sometimes wondered if he had died.

Then just before Christmas 2018 a letter came:

Dear Alice

You may or may not remember me. I met you in Lough Derg, many, many years ago. We talked about priests' homilies. You said that they were too long and not topical. We had a long discussion and I asked you to write to me in Cork. I don't remember whether you did or not. I was in Innishannon for the launching of the O'Connell monument.

I am now in an Augustinian nursing home, aged 99, immobile and unable to do anything. I had a very busy and active life, 30 years in New Ross as teacher and principal of Good Counsel College, 12 years in Galway, 4 years in Cork, 4 years in Limerick. I gave mission retreats all over the country … I have read all your books … and am reading your latest book *And Life Lights Up*. You are blessed and gifted with a mixture of the natural and divine. Your language is so simple and poetic. You have such attention to detail. Well done thou good and faithful servant. You have nourished the lives of so many people. Please forgive my writing, it happens when one reaches 99. I have had a very full and happy life. Now I await the last moment of my life. I hope that we shall meet in heaven. Continue your good work. *Beannacht Dé agus na Maighdine Muire ar do chuid oibre.* I shall continue to read your books, say my prayers during Advent and prepare for Christmas.

Love, Blessings and Gratitude

Grá, Beannachtaí agus Buiochas

Fr Jackie Power O. S. A.

I was absolutely delighted to hear from this man, who, though we had only met on two occasions, had had a big influence on my life. I wrote to him before

Christmas and told him so. Then early in the New Year I heard that he had died. With his arrival, heaven will be a brighter place. Hopefully, as he wished, we will meet again for a third time.

Many Milestones

I am not big into birthdays. They pass me by like ships in the night, my own and others, sometimes much to the annoyance of others. I blame my mother! Birthdays came and went in our house and she made no big deal of them. For years I thought that my birthday was on the 8th of February only to discover when I applied for a birth certificate that it was, in fact, on the 28th February. My mother was mildly surprised to discover that she had got it wrong, but assured me that a few days one way or the other was neither here nor there. Her happy-go-lucky approach to birthdays resulted in the practice that when my eldest was a toddler and a suitable sunny day dawned, I would announce to his delight that this was his birthday, open the garden gate, send out an SOS around the village and in no time at all we had an impromptu birthday party. No formal invitations, no presents, just cake and ice-cream and fun and games around the garden. This worked and was a great success for many years when they were all very young. Then, before I

Sincere
Wishes
on your
BIRTHDAY

I wish for you in all sincerity
Joy, health, and luck,
and much prosperity.
V. M. E.

413

could be found out, I changed tactics and complied with normality. Could those impromptu parties have been called surprise birthday parties?

Over the years I have been moulded into dutifully complying with forward planning. And this year in Innishannon was the final nail in the coffin of my cavalier attitude to birthdays. The village had three big birthdays to mark – so big were they that it was decided that the term 'birthday' did not quite cover the significance of these occasions, so it got changed to 'milestones'. So we had three big milestones to mark! Firstly, the Parish Hall had been built by voluntary labour in 1968, so it was fifty years old. Then the Tidy Towns group was founded in 1968 by four stalwarts: Rev Matchette, Bromley Rohu, Margaret O'Sullivan and my late husband Gabriel, so it was the same age. And our annual Christmas magazine *Candlelight* was on its 35th edition. So this was, in many ways, a very special year for Innishannon and it was felt that we should do something to celebrate these three milestones. And work had been in progress on a brochure of Leisure Walks around Innishannon which was nearing completion, so we needed a launch pad for that as well.

But we kept putting it on the long finger, and as Christmas drew nearer, I half-hoped that the celebrations to mark the milestones would get forgotten. But

not so, not so! Joe, our Tidy Towns treasurer, had, with
relentless determination, got stuck into it and jet-
propelled it forward, and with his enthusiasm he had
ignited others. He pointed out that as all these milestones occurred in 2018 they should be celebrated
within that year. I half-heartedly went along with it
and as I had all the back photo albums of the Tidy
Towns activities over the years and the back numbers
of *Candlelight* stored up in my attic, there was almost
no choice but to get involved. And gradually, in spite
of my reluctance, I got caught up in the enthusiasm –
and the fact that the night of celebrations was scheduled for right before Christmas, which previously I
perceived as a disadvantage, now became a bonus. It
would open the door into Christmas.

The local GAA club were having their annual Big
Christmas Breakfast in the Parish Hall that morning,
so it was the afternoon before we got possession of the
hall, but the club had left it spick and span. So we got
ready our Christmas tree, which Catherine, our local
florist from Petals and Presents, had decorated and the
beautiful tree now got pride of place in front of the
stage. Catherine had also brought along some of her
tall candelabra, which she normally uses for weddings,
and now they added a sense of grandeur. The plan
was to have four large tables around the hall: one for
the celebration of fifty years of Tidy Towns activities,

one to commemorate the building of the Parish Hall, one for *Candlelight* and another for the launch of the new Leisure Walks. Each table was draped with a large, fancy tablecloth and adorned with candelabra borrowed from the local church. The Tidy Towns table was laden with photo albums of all the activities over the years, the Parish Hall table with every old photo and artefact that we could gather from around the parish. On the *Candlelight* table we had a candle, and fanned around it all the back numbers of *Candlelight*. There were bound volumes of the back numbers as well. The Leisure Walk table had brochures and maps of the planned walks.

On tables along the bottom of the hall, Deirdre, from our local café, the Found Out, would do the catering, and Breda, a woman for all occasions, would serve mulled wine from a table at the entrance, filling the hall with a festive aroma. When the whole layout was complete, the hall looked great. We were all ready to go.

That night, when people poured into the hall, they made a beeline for all the old photos and pored over them, with much laughter and remembering. Many of the photos were of children who were now adults and they had great fun identifying themselves and others. Some people had been part of the volunteer teams who had built the hall, and they chatted and reminisced. In many ways it was a very nostalgic occasion and, as we had hoped, it was Old Innishannon remembering and New Innishannon getting to know the history of this place that was now their place as well. The red velvet stage curtains were closed and fronted by lighted candles, so all the activities were down in the hall, creating a greater sense of togetherness.

Paudie, who was in charge of proceedings, got us going and our local River Rhythms choir sang us off to a great start with Christmas carols. Then Tidy Towns opened proceedings with a summary by Margaret, who was a founder member, of how it all began, and the story was continued by Peter, the current chairman. Then on to the Parish Hall, and Kit read a poem written at the time of the actual building by local man Jer Desmond.

Jer had read his ballad fifty years earlier on the night of the opening of the hall and we had later recorded it in *Candlelight*, which was just as well, as otherwise the words of it would have gone into the grave with Jer. To build a Parish Hall in today's Ireland with voluntary labour would be inconceivable, but fifty years ago that posed no problem. For many present, it was a surprise to learn how their hall had been built. As Kit read the poem, typical of its time, the old natives smiled in remembrance and the newcomers were surprised and amused. Here's an extract:

As Time Goes By

As we meet here tonight we are thrilled with delight
In opening this beautiful hall
Well, it is only true that 'twas well overdue
But we hadn't a chew that was all.
'Twas a fortunate gale blew up from Kinsale
Father Riordan to hail as a friend,
He could cut out red tape and put things into shape
We were soon on a great upward trend.

Amongst things great and small he got at the dance hall
And we knew he was on the right track
He said, 'Now boys be here, bring your sledges and gear,
And we'll start to pull down the old shack.'
Well, the work did proceed at astonishing speed
A fresh team each night was the plan
Gabriel would appear like a head engineer
And he made Connors a permanent man.

Excavation took place for a sound solid base
And McCarthy's bulldozer did bark
Then after excavation we put down the foundation
And worked every night until dark ...

Now the hall is complete, it is noble and neat
'Tis the pride of the village so grand
From Cork to Dungannon no place like Innishannon
The loveliest place in the land.
By the hall you could dream amid woodland and stream
And the beautiful bridge of renown
You've the garage by Phil at the foot of the hill
And the Parson above looking down.

It was strange to hear this poem that had first been read on the opening night by Jer himself repeated now fifty years later. Many of the people mentioned in it were no longer with us and it was wonderful to remember them all and their great contributions. It made one realise the importance of recording parish events as they happen, as otherwise they get lost as the years go by.

As we were coming back from that trip down memory lane, beautiful Linda Kenny, who lives in the parish and whose wonderful voice has graced the National Concert Hall and the Cork Opera House, took the microphone and lit up the hall with her sunny smile and amazing voice. You could sense delight ooze around the hall. Then it was my turn to tell the gathering about the origins and journey of *Candlelight* over the past thirty-five years. And then on to Joe to tell us all about the brochures and Leisure Walks around the parish. The seed for these walks had actually been planted by my husband Gabriel, who was a great walker, and many years previously had written a detailed article in *Candlelight* about the walks, including the times and distances involved in doing them. It was strange how many simple parish activities can in later years bear a rich harvest. Then back to Linda, who led the crowd in song. It was one of those nights that flowed with effortless ease and the hall was full of delighted faces.

That, I thought, is that! And what a great night it had turned out to be despite my original reluctance to have it so close to Christmas.

Then, much to my surprise, Diarmuid, who was not part of the plan for the night, took the microphone. And here he was, detailing all the activities that I myself had been involved with in the parish since my arrival there in 1961. To me it came as a complete bombshell. I was gob-smacked. Nobody had divulged that this was about to happen. It was the hidden agenda of the night, and it came completely out of the blue.

They presented me with a magnificent basket of flowers, a clock crafted in bog oak from my home valley and a framed certificate of appreciation indicating the planting of an oak tree in a location of my choice in the village. Then my niece, Treasa, who had been hiding in the crowd lest she raise my suspicions, came to the microphone and sang a Christmas carol that my brother Tim had written years previously and each year is now sung in our home church on Christmas night. Then, to conclude, she led us all in singing 'Silent Night'.

It was a beautiful, heart-warming and wonderful occasion. Usually people have to die to enjoy such an event!

As I walked home along the village the words of WB Yeats came to mind:

Think where man's glory most begins and ends
And say my glory was I had such friends.

* * *

Months later when my oak tree was planted it triggered off the creation of a Memory Grove in the village. People who wanted to celebrate a special occasion, or to remember a loved one, brought along a tree to be planted. We have a large sloped area in the village from where many dead trees had been removed, and it was lying idle. People liked the idea of planting a tree in memory of someone and slowly the area is filling up with memory trees.

As Time Goes By

A Memory Tree

Plant a tree in memory of me
And for hundreds of years
My tree will bless the earth.

Within its many branches
Birds will build their nests
Bees will find rich nectar
My roots will drain the earth
and my leaves cleanse the air.

So please plant a tree
To shelter future generations
And life will live in the sacred space
Created by the tree you plant.

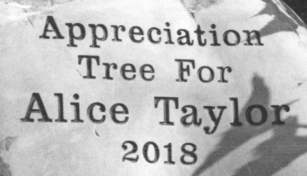

Appreciation
Tree For
Alice Taylor
2018

Tidy Towns

As Time Goes By

When I was twenty I thought I knew everything and now that I am eighty I have learned that, in actual fact, I know very little. GB Shaw is said to have declared that 'Youth is wasted on the young', but maybe that proclamation could be applied to all stages of our lives. Often we don't appreciate where we are in life. In my middle years I was on a parish-hall building committee with a wise old priest who asked me before one meeting to second a motion that he would propose, and I protested angrily saying that that was not democracy. He looked at me with wise, kindly eyes, and said gently, 'Alice, girleen, you have an awful lot to learn.' How right he was! And I am still learning.

I suppose each generation feels it has seen huge changes, but one scene from my childhood illustrates for me one enormous change that my generation has seen. Back when I was going to school through the fields we walked across a little bridge in the morning and put a stone on it to record that we had passed.

The stone was there to let the next family who came along the valley know that we had gone on ahead. Each family had their own stone. Looking back now, I realise that that stone was our way of communicating. In a sense, it was our first telephone. A stone telephone! And now we are on the internet with access to the whole world at the tip of our finger. That is a big leap for one generation. Aren't we are great to be coping so well?

I sometimes smile at some of our reactions to certain new developments as they came. When the first radio, a large weighty contraption powered by two heavy glass batteries, was introduced to our house, its home was on the deep sill of the window on the back wall of our kitchen, which it filled. Because house walls were thick, the window sills were deep and spacious. When it was first turned on, we small children were mesmerised to hear strange voices come out of this new brown box booming forth from the window sill above our heads. We actually went out the front door and made our way around to the back of the house to see if this strange man talking to us was hiding there!

But that radio opened up a whole new world for us, or rather, brought the wider world into our world. There were just two stations, BBC and Raidio Éireann, and my father quickly became an ardent BBC listener, fascinated by their news bulletins and weather forecasts, while my mother opted for Raidio Éireann, which she felt was nearer to her traditional Irish values. But even she was enticed to abandon Raidio Éireann for 'Woman's Hour' and 'Mrs Dale's Diary' on the BBC. We children became addicted to the 'Dick Barton Special Agent' detective series featuring Dick, Snowey and Jack every night at 6.45 on the BBC. Then, unimaginable in today's world, once a week the whole country tuned into *céilí* dancing classes on Raidio Éireann with Din Joe on 'Take the Floor', when we could hear the stamping of dancing shoes off the floor. Dancing on the radio! We too took to the floor and followed Din Joe's instructions around our kitchen. 'Question Time' with Joe Linnane tested our general knowledge, and 'Around the Fire' entertained us as we sat around our own fire. I can still remember the haunting voice of Sean Ó Síocháin singing the 'The Boys of Barr na Sráide as they hunted for the Wran'. We loved the plays on the BBC and were faithful listeners to 'Book at Bedtime'. There for the first time I heard *The Tale of Two Cities* being read, and I never forgot the opening lines: 'It was the best of times. It was the worst of times.' Those words are as applicable today as then. Later, Radio Luxembourg came on air and a whole new pop culture swam into our teenage world, with Elvis Presley's

'Wooden Heart' setting our young hearts thumping with delight.

On Sunday afternoons the thrilling voice of Micheál O'Hehir, with his graphic descriptions of matches and players, turned our kitchen into Croke Park. When my brother set up a boxing club in our barn we listened to the commentary on boxing contests from all over the world and became familiar with the difference between heavyweight, lightweight, featherweight, bantamweight, and with names like Joe Louis, Bruce Woodcock and Rinty Monaghan. We also followed with interest the extraordinary career of Jack Doyle, the 'Gorgeous Gael', who, amongst his many colourful pursuits, turned his hand – or rather his fists – to boxing. Recently, amidst a little controversy, they erected a monument to him in his native Cobh. It was in some ways a bit like welcoming home the prodigal son.

When electricity came to our home place in 1956 this large radio and the glass batteries became redundant, so we no longer had to walk the three miles into town to get them charged. But probably the two electrical items that brought the greatest ease to household chores was the electric kettle and the iron. The kettle could be plugged in for a quick cup of tea before early-morning milking, and the wonderful electric iron replaced the little monster of a box iron, which would scorch all around it if not in capable hands. At first, people did not think of getting an electric cooker or a washing machine as, in the early days of electricity, these were considered comforts beyond reach – our town cousins were ahead of us culchies in acquiring these luxuries. But gradually, electrical items found their way into all our homes and made life much easier. But frugal living was still the practice of the time and there were very few luxuries in our homes, and we were really experts at 'making do'. There was very little waste as all leftover food was fed to the animals, and the land was nourished by horse and cow dung. Unknowingly, we were masters of the art of what is now known as the 'living inside the gate' philosophy, which was surely a major preventive of global warming.

When I look back now I realise that though we had never heard of recycling, composting, caring for the environment or organic farming, we were, in fact, practising them all. There was no such thing as disposable anything, and the plague of plastic had yet to come. The corncrake was the night chorus and the cuckoo visited every April. Because spraying crops with chemicals was unheard of, our bee population had no limits put to their flight and every Sunday my father fished the river on our farm, and that evening when my mother opened up the trout there were no unsavoury bits within. In those days we depended on nature, now it depends on us. Over the years, our world has made amazing progress in many areas, but unfortunately in some we were not as environmentally aware as we should have been, and we and our children could pay a terrible price for our lack of caring for the needs of the earth.

Some years ago we had programme on TV called 'Mission Impossible', in which agents were issued with instructions about a proposed mission and the tape concluded with the message: 'In three seconds this tape will self-destruct.' Now as I listen to the dire warning about the plight of our planet and the threat to our marine and bee life, I wonder if the plight of the fish and bees will not also be ours. Words of my father echo down the years to me: 'Wrong nature and you pay a terrible price.' Not a comforting prospect!

But, on the other hand, there are no limits to the resilience and capability of the human spirit. Should we put our minds to it and decide to grasp the problem that we have created, and all put our shoulder to the wheel, surely we can transform our world. It is in our hands. We can learn from our past mistakes and transform our future.

Also from Alice Taylor

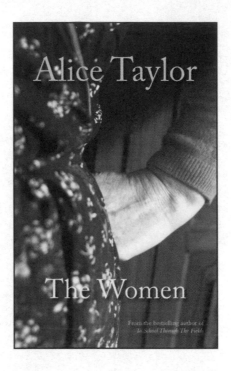

'In these pages, we see Taylor's remarkable gift of elevating the ordinary to something special, something poetic, even ... Like all of her books, it's a thing of gentle beauty.'
Irish Independent

We walk in the footprints of great women, women who lived through hard times on farms, in villages, towns and cities. The lives of these women are an untold story. This book is a celebration of the often forgotten 'ordinary' women who gave so much to our society.

Alice Taylor salutes the women whose energy and generosity made such a valuable contribution to all our lives.

'Alice Taylor guides us through the steps and ways to live a conscious life and focus on the goodness of the world around us.'
Belfast Telegraph

There are special moments in everyone's life. They can happen in the most ordinary circumstances and wake us up to the joy of living. In this heart-warming book Alice Taylor celebrates such experiences in all their variety – taking the time to notice the beauty of a flower, listening attentively to a piece of music, appreciating someone's small act of kindness, celebrating creativity through gardening, wood carving, knitting, sewing.

It's all about being in the moment and being aware of the magic as it happens. In this way we enrich our everyday living and create an inner reservoir of golden moments. This reservoir of special times is a treasure to be cherished.

**'A must for those of you who like to put their feet up in front of the fire
and read about the joys of Christmas.'**
The Kerryman

With all the warmth of a winter fire, Alice takes us through the exciting
preparation for Christmas, from getting the perfect tree to baking those crucial
puddings and pies. She gives us an intimate insight into her Christmas Eve and
Christmas day rituals and talks us through her favourite Christmas recipes. She
tells how the Christmas foods were made when she was a child, using the bastable
and the range, and how she prepares them now.

Alice loves Christmas, and her huge enjoyment of the season fills this book with
pleasure and delight.

See more books by Alice Taylor at www.obrien.ie